PLAYING HOUSE

IN

PROVENCE

PLAYING HOUSE IN

PROVENCE

How Two Americans Became
a Little Bit French

Mary-Lou Weisman

PLAYING HOUSE IN PROVENCE
HOW TWO AMERICANS BECAME A LITTLE BIT FRENCH

iUniverse books may be ordered through booksellers or by contacting:

iUniverse
1663 Liberty Drive
Bloomington, IN 47403
www.iuniverse.com
1-800-Authors (1-800-288-4677)

Because of the dynamic nature of the Internet, any web addresses or links contained in this book may have changed since publication and may no longer be valid. The views expressed in this work are solely those of the author and do not necessarily reflect the views of the publisher, and the publisher hereby disclaims any responsibility for them.

Any people depicted in stock imagery provided by Thinkstock are models, and such images are being used for illustrative purposes only.
Certain stock imagery © Thinkstock.

ISBN: 978-1-5320-2534-1 (sc)
ISBN: 978-1-5320-2535-8 (e)

Library of Congress Control Number: 2017909067

Print information available on the last page.

iUniverse rev. date: 09/01/2017

Wherever we roam
With Larry, I'm home

Changing Places

I don't know about you, but no matter where we're traveling, especially if we're having a wonderful time, we invariably stop at the local Realtor's office to peer at the listings and indulge in a one-month rental fantasy. We choose the house we like best, convert the price from euros to dollars, and then fly home and forget entirely about our dream until our next one-week vacation.

My husband, Larry, and I don't want to tour a foreign country; we want to become part of it. We want to pierce the tourist veil, get as close to the essence of the culture as we can. No more observing from the outside, our noses pressed to the glass. We yearn for someone to open the door and invite us to step right in and make ourselves at home. To accomplish this would take time, more than the week we usually allot for a vacation.

It took decades before we put our fantasy to the test of reality. By then, both of us were in our low sixties, right on the cusp of being late middle-aged and young-old. But since sixty had just become the new fifty, perhaps we were merely late middle-aged. We had raised our children. We had solidified our careers. We had saved enough money so that we could travel. We were still in pretty good shape, probably because we enjoy physical activity. We swim. We ride bikes. We hike. We have arthritis. We pump up the volume on the TV. We are beginning to hear from our rotator cuffs. Couldn't we have at least one last great adventure before all we can do is try to balance on our walkers on the decks of cruise ships?

We had been playing this game of fantasy *interruptus* for years until one day, in the lovely Provençal town of L'Isle-sur-la-Sorgue (sounds like Leel sur la Sorg), our fantasy caught up with us.

The year was 2002. We were strolling in the shade of the romantic plane trees, past the huge, mossy paddles of the ancient wooden waterwheels that churn at the river below. We stopped for coffee at Le Café Bellevue, where the Sorgue River swells to the size of a small lake and ducks paddle sweetly by. We talked about how much fun it would be to shed the twenty-first century and live in this medieval town.

This was hardly a new conversation for us; it was just a new medieval town. We talked about how we'd rent a little house, buy cheeses and pâtés at the market, drink wine at lunch, tuck baguettes under our arms, and pedal our bikes to Le Café Bellevue, where we'd be regulars, and eventually they'd like us, even though we're Americans. In time, we would become so French that we wouldn't like Americans either.

"But we couldn't just hang out for a month," I said. "We'd have to find something to do, some way to connect. We could take a French course."

"Or maybe a cooking class," suggested Larry, who always has food on his mind.

One would have thought, given our record for unrealized rental fantasies, that neither of us would have dared to say, "Wouldn't it be great to live here for a while?" But one of us did.

Just then we saw the sign posted on a telephone pole: *"Cours de français. Immersion Totale."* We took the sign literally, as a sign. We would immerse ourselves totally in the study of French.

We both love the French language, and we already had a head start. Larry had studied French for three years in high school. Then he spent the summer after his first year of college riding his Vespa all over Europe, ending up in Paris, where he registered for a course at the Sorbonne, which entitled him to a cheap dorm room at La Cité Universitaire. He may have attended a class or two—he certainly meant to—but mostly he hung out in cafés, hitting on French women.

I, too, had studied French for three years in high school. The source of my love for France and the French language is Oedipal. My father loved words. It was important to him that I not settle for less than the right word. *"Cherchez le mot just,"* my father insisted, even when I was a little kid, writing book reports in grade school. He knew a few French words and phrases and enjoyed decorating his conversation with a *bon mot* whenever he got the chance. I grew up believing it was important to be able to speak French—or at least to be able to fake it. We were thus primed to choose France for our first experiment in international living.

I groped in my pocketbook to write down the e-mail address on the *cours français* sign—bringing our fantasy one step closer to reality—but could find only paper, no pencil.

"Excusez-moi," said Larry to a good-looking, middle-aged man with a fetching black moustache, who was sitting on the nearby curb, sanding a bureau. *"Avez-vous un crayon?"* The man put down his work, stood up, and begrudgingly made his way to the house in front of which he had been seated. He returned shortly with a pencil. After a quick *"Merci,"* Larry turned and began copying the e-mail address on the sign.

"Ne partez pas, ne partez pas, attendez un moment," cried the man. He was asking us not to leave. Our vestigial French was holding up. So far, so *bon.*

This time, the man we would come to know as Ange dashed into his house and returned with Monique Desrozier, his pretty, vivacious lover and the woman with whom we would be totally immersed for three of our four stays in Provence, each a month long, over the next four years. She would also turn out to be our coconspirator in the heady but perilous plot of pretending to be French.

Our fantasy was taking on some flesh-and-blood reality. She invited us into her home, where a third-floor room served as her classroom. She spoke to us exclusively in French and yet chose her words carefully and pronounced them with such precision that we understood almost everything she said. At that moment, it was easy to imagine living in this beautiful town and studying in this classroom with this charming woman. I put the piece of paper with her name and e-mail address in my pocketbook and hesitated, searching my mind for the right way to say goodbye. Even people who haven't studied French know about *adieu, au revoir,* and *voulez-vous coucher avec moi,* but there was a better word, and I couldn't find it.

"*A bientôt,*" Monique said.

Of course. See you soon. That was it.

"*A bientôt,*" we replied, and off we went, giddy with excitement and promise. But did we mean it? Were we just teasing or were we going to go all the way? At the time, even we didn't know.

The moment of truth came a couple of days later when we were back home. After emptying out our suitcases and sorting our clothes into piles of lights and darks, I turned my attention to my pocketbook. I put my passport back in my desk drawer, stashed the extra euros in a Ziploc bag, crumpled up all the used tissues, my boarding pass, and the ads for underwater watches and foot massagers I'd torn out of *Sky Mall* magazine, and tossed them into the trash. Then I came upon the scrap of paper on which Larry had written Monique Desrozier's e-mail address. It took me a moment to realize what I was holding. Now that we were home, sated by a week of travel in France and eager to resume our lives, how foolish, never mind how unnecessary and potentially disappointing the pursuit of this fantasy could be. I knew better. I was about to crumple and toss the address into the basket when I thought about a conversation I once had with my father, just after he'd retired. A man of steady habits, he confided to me that he had long harbored a most peculiar fantasy, to be a butler in a well-run household. I asked him why he didn't fulfill his fantasy. After all, there was nothing to stop him. "But if I did," he explained, "then I wouldn't have the fantasy, would I?"

How wise I thought him at the time! Fantasy, by definition, is an idea that has no basis in reality. Yet such is its lure that we nurture it in spite of what we know to be true. I found myself wondering: Maybe my father *would* have been a happy butler. Maybe you *can* have your fantasy and eat it too, so to speak.

Then we worried about money. The euro was on the rise against the dollar. We knew that the days when we could travel in Europe on five dollars a day were long gone, but Provence on $150 a day?

Between Larry's second and third years of law school, we camped throughout Europe on even less than five dollars a day. We funded this adventure with money we received as wedding gifts, which is why we still have no silver flatware or china. We never missed them. We're not much for luxuries. In Europe, we cooked over a Coleman stove. It took forty-five minutes to get the water for spaghetti to boil. In Italy, we drank a red wine called Est Est Est, which cost less than a Coke. In the Loire Valley, we bought an *entrecôte*, which we thought was a steak, and cooked it over a campground fire. It *was* a steak, a very chewy horse steak. We buried it, commemorating the event with a cross made of twigs and a homemade sign reading "Dobbin, RIP." That night we shared tuna from a can.

When we were in Rome, our financial situation got desperate. I horrified Larry by plunging my right arm in up to the elbow, stealing loose change from many a public fountain. Robbing some naive coin-tossers of their wishes bothered me a lot less than the prospect of skipping lunch. I drew the line at the Vatican fountain.

In Tours, France, we washed in the public baths after a sign on the shower in the campgrounds informed us that the shower wasn't working. *"La douche ne marche pas."* When you're poor in France, a lot of things don't *marche.* I sat naked on a long, slatted wooden bench, waiting my turn with a lot of other naked women, who were also getting stripe marks on their buttocks, until a matron carrying a stack of towels and tiny bars of soap escorted us to the women's shower room. There, one pull of a rope would get you a couple of seconds of hot water to soap up, and a second pull would allow you to rinse off. Then, shivering, we dried ourselves with towels so frayed we could see through them. A sign on the shower wall read, *"Défense de chanter et siffler."* Singing and whistling are prohibited. As if.

Poverty is a reliable way to find your way into a culture without even trying. It ensures that you will have experiences denied to most tourists. Still, with the accumulation of money, age, and an increased desire for creature comforts, poverty has lost its charms. We no longer like to shower in public or sleep outdoors in a bag.

The amount of money it would cost us to fund this month was staggering, but Larry, the major moneymaker, was unshaken. He had not yet retired, but he had achieved enough seniority at his law firm that he could take a month-long vacation without raising eyebrows. Besides, he was certain he could sustain his clients on virtual life support, plugged into his cell phone. Money would still be coming in, and I could write anywhere.

We decided that September would be the best time to be in Provence—not too hot, yet early enough to avoid the cold blasts of the mistral winds that come from the north and typically arrive by early October, although they can happen at any time.

I went to my computer, English/French dictionary in hand, and composed an e-mail telling Mme Desrozier that we'd like to study French with her three times a week during the entire month of September and asked her if she would please give us the name of a Realtor who could find us a house in L'Isle sur La Sorgue. That bit of prose alone required several dictionary consults. I returned one last time to the dictionary's "Useful Phrases Section" to figure out how to sign off. Nothing simple and straightforward like "Sincerely" was apparent, so I chose the shortest option, *Dans l'attente de votre réponse*—I look forward to hearing from you—and hit send. I was already pretending to be French.

Now that we had found a teacher, we needed to find a house, some place modest but comfortable. We were determined to live in L'Isle sur la Sorgue so that we could walk to Monique's house from Le Café Bellevue. Within a day or two, I received a response from Monique. *"Je suis ravie,"* it began. Uh oh. Was she raving? Was she ravenous? I had pretended too well. I went back to the dictionary. No, she was merely delighted. This would be the first of many encounters with annoyingly deceptive French words.

Monique also provided us with contact information for a Realtor, Catherine Gottinkiene. I wrote her an e-mail, also in tediously researched French, spelling out our needs. She responded with a contract, which took a half hour to translate, describing a house on a street called Impasse des Jardins, a dead-end street and gardens. The place sounded appealing, and it seemed to fulfill our requirements at a price we could afford, although barely.

In order to get to Provence, we first fly from JKF Airport in New York to Charles de Gaulle Airport in Paris and then board a train for Avignon. From there, we pick up our rental car and drive to L'Isle sur la Sorgue. During the six-hour plane trip, Larry, a borderline narcoleptic, falls asleep before the flight attendant has a chance to demonstrate how to fasten a seat belt, and he continues to sleep soundly through the entire trip. I, an insomniac, having taken two Ambien, remain paradoxically wide awake and unjustifiably furious with Larry.

Once in Charles de Gaulle, we are instantly reminded that we are tourists. We cannot find any signs at any of the *portes* or gates that read "Avignon." I flip through the pages of my yellow 3 x 4–inch English-French/French-English dictionary.

"*Où est la porte pour Avignon?*" I ask some guy I'm pretty sure is French since I couldn't fit into his shirt. Frenchmen tend to be small, wiry, and two-dimensional. He directs us to a gate, the sign over which reads "Marseille." I've heard that Parisians can be perverse, but are they sadistic enough to purposely sabotage strangers? Then after a moment, Larry, who knows east from west the second he emerges from a New York subway, gets it. Avignon is in the *direction* of Marseille.

Boarding the high-speed train, familiarly known as the TGV or *train à grande vitesse,* is *une comédie d'erreurs* unless it's happening to you. You can't just get on any old first- or second-class wagon. You must get on a specific car and then into a specific seat. It says so on our ticket, but we can't read our ticket because it's in French. Some of the information is clear enough; we know we're in *seconde classe,* but we can't decipher the rest. We also don't understand that the TGV, in order to maintain its reputation for *grande vitesse,* will bullet into the station, soundlessly open its silver doors, take a few deep, electronic breaths, close its doors, and speed on toward its target, Marseille. If you're left behind, it's too bad. *Tant pis.*

We barely have time to lug ourselves and our baggage onto the wrong car before the doors slide shut. The conductor expels us at the next stop where we must leap, along with our baggage, onto the platform below and run like crazy to the right car and scramble aboard before the doors hiss closed again.

One near death experience averted, we await the next. It turns out to be driving. We pick up our rental car at the Avignon station. Larry, who is by far the more confident driver and has a much better sense of direction takes the wheel and maneuvers out of the parking lot and onto the roadway. Within a kilometer, the traffic in front of us slows to a crawl and we find ourselves facing a road sign that reads, *"Vous N'avez Pas La Priorité."* Literally, you do not have the priority. This is not meant to be an existential French statement about the meaning of life; all it means is "yield." We will see this sign whenever we are approaching a *rond-point*. Rotaries, rather than red lights, are the way the French control traffic. Only *their* rotaries aren't puny little "here we go round the mulberry bush" American traffic circles. A French rotary is *la maman* of all rotaries with exits at regular intervals, like rays from a giant sunburst.

Larry inches along in line. When it's his turn to enter, he leans forward, trains his eyes to the left toward the oncoming traffic circling the rotary, and waits for an opening. As soon as Larry sees one car exit, he guns into the newly created space, which is about the size of a car length, and I let out my breath. We go around the rotary, reading the exit signs for various towns, hoping for one that reads *"Direction L'Isle sur la Sorgue."* We drive around again and again while I consult the map until I have determined that none of the towns named on the exit signs are going to take us to L'Isle; not "Arles," not "Nîmes," not "Centre Ville," and not "La Barthellasse." The only other option, besides driving around in circles chasing other people's tail pipes until we run out of gas, is to exit at a wild card of a sign that we've been rejecting because we've been taking it too literally: *"Toutes Directions."* All Directions. They really mean all *other* directions. Larry turns on his blinker, and off we go in all directions. We drive through the town of Le Pontet on the outskirts of Avignon. We have chosen wisely, if desperately. After a few more minutes, a few more rotaries, and a few more *Toutes Directions,* we see the exit option for L'Isle sur la Sorgue.

We're headed in the right direction.

We turn on the car radio. Neither of us understands a word.

We pass a storefront sign that reads in big, red letters, "Pain."

"Imagine how baffled you'd be if you didn't know it meant *bread,*" I remark, regaining my confidence after a series of Franco-flops.

A precedent has been set that we don't yet realize. For the next month, we will be temporarily bipolar, our moods swinging between the yin of failure and the yang of success.

We are jet-lagged, we are tense, and in just a few minutes, *grâce à Dieu,* we will arrive at Impasse des Jardins, our home. We imagine a little charmer of a cottage, surrounded by flowers, on a dead-end street.

We imagine wrong. It is hate at first sight. Other than the obvious fact that the house is located in Provence, there is nothing Provençal about this yellowing plaster rectangle that looks like a crumbling hunk of parmesan cheese, located in a development of identical, shabby rectangles.

Upon further inspection, we hate it more. Where are the plane trees, the sunflowers, the cunning eaves, the dark Provençal beams and the terra-cotta tile floors we had come to love when we were tourists in Provence? The well-named *impasse* turns out to be a dead-end alley so narrow that Larry can barely drive down it without knocking the side mirrors off our rental car.

The *jardin* is a total misnomer. No grass or flowers could possibly grow on this small plot of parched earth in the middle of what can only be called, at least by American standards, a subdivision. There is no shower—not even a metered one. The two-burner stove and tiny oven are encrusted with food. The owner's products fill the ice-bound freezer. Is Larry, who loves to cook as well as eat, supposed to make *boeuf bourguignon* in this dump of a kitchen?

We realize too late how critical real estate is to our Provençal experiment. We had imagined a nicely renovated house with some age to it, at least a century or two. I feel sick with disappointment and dread. What have we done? What can we do about it? Meanwhile, Mme Gottinkiene stands by, waiting, hands on her hips, tapping her toe.

I am at a loss for words, except for *"Impossible!"* which I pronounce loudly in my best French accent. Lots of words in the French language are the same, as long as you send them through your nose.

Mme Gottinkiene, who speaks English better than we speak French, reminds us that we will forfeit our hefty deposit if we do not take the house. Then she goes on to accuse us of being typical spoiled-rotten Americans.

That does it for me. I don't like being accused of being typical. I don't know where I find the words to confront her, or why I choose to address her in French. I may have been trying to prove to her how wrong she was about us. Typical Americans don't speak French, even bad French. My tone is at once aggressive and heartfelt. I explain to an astounded Realtor that Larry and I have been dreaming of living in Provence for years, that we love the French people, their language, and their style of living, that we have come here for a month, that we are going to study French four hours a day, three days a week with Monique Desroziers, and that we will not under any circumstances live in this nightmare of a house. She can keep our deposit. We will look elsewhere. To this day, Larry calls it my "I Have a Dream" speech.

By the time I get done, the expression on her face has changed from total disdain to loving-kindness. Is it the touching eloquence of my broken but earnest French? Or is it the mention of Monique Desroziers, who, as luck would have it, is Catherine's friend?

We repair to a nearby café to talk things over. L'Isle sur la Sorgue, she explains, for all its Venetian charm, its lovely cafes, antique shops, and waterwheels, is a blue-collar town with very few rental properties. People stay put. The reality of an ugly, circa 1950 French ranch house never occurred to me.

My tendency to confuse fantasy with reality will continue to be both a blessing and a curse.

If we are willing to live outside of L'Isle sur la Sorgue, she will find us a suitable house. Furthermore, she will see to it that we don't have to forfeit our deposit on the house we have rejected; nor will she take her commission. By the time we have consumed enough café to send the three of us to the bathroom numerous times, we have learned that Catherine used to be a Catholic, but now she is a Buddhist.

"There are no bad experiences," Catherine says. "Difficulties are good," she adds, nearly convincing us that renting a rotten house in the wrong town was an excellent choice on our part. She then gives us an example from her own life.

She used to be married to a German man with whom she'd had a daughter in Germany. He took up with another woman, got her pregnant, and left Catherine. According to some legalism we don't understand, in order for Catherine to return to France, she had to leave her daughter with her ex-husband in Germany for an entire year.

"This was the hardest thing I ever did," she says. Still, after a year, her daughter chose to be with her, and now Catherine lives with her daughter and Yves, the man who helped her to make the transition from Germany to France. They had started out as friends, and now they are a couple. Catherine will be our first French friend. She makes short work of finding us a perfect house six kilometers from L'Isle sur la Sorgue in Saumane de Vaucluse, a small village perched on the top of a hill, *un village perché*, with an adorably tiny population of 820, including Catherine, Yves, and her daughter. Now 822, counting us. The house even comes with two bikes, which we are free to use during our stay.

In the First Place

Home Sweet Medieval Home

It is September 2003 when we first see our house on rue de L'Eglise and immediately put our fantasy of riding bikes down the treacherous hill to Le Café Bellevue on hold. It won't be our first fantasy to hit the dust. So what if we will have to drive six kilometers each morning down the winding, serpentine hillside road that leads to L'Isle sur la Sorgue below.

The house is just right—a medieval, attached townhouse with cunning shutters and a heavy, planked wooden front door, located directly on a narrow street meant for carriages, not cars. The house is so old that the plumbing's on the outside. My heart leaps when Catherine takes a large, toothy key out of her purse, the kind that might have hung from the belt of a Shakespearean chambermaid, and opens the door.

The inside of the house is just as appealing. We enter onto a small landing from which two steps lead down to what Catherine calls the "salon." To us, *salon* summons up a gathering of bright and witty, high-bosomed women, one of them Mme de Sévigné, lying about, holding forth on an encyclopedia of subjects. But those Renaissance days are over. These days, French salons are merely living rooms, and this one is comfortably furnished with an attractive mix of contemporary and antique chairs, a sofa and a glass coffee table. The kitchen is very small but modern and well equipped. There are no closets in the two bedrooms—only armoires. We have a wall of sliding-door closets at home, but here we love armoires; they're old, inconvenient, and hardly hold anything. And the floors are terra-cotta. On the very distressed, antique dining room table stands a bottle of champagne, along with a note from the owners, which reads in sweetly broken English, "Have a nice days." Buddhism is beginning to look good.

Unlike our town, where a street named Bonnie Brook Lane doesn't necessarily have a brook, rue de L'Eglise has a church, the tiny, chaste twelfth-century Romanesque church of St. Trophime, built against the town's ramparts, with a view of the colorful patchwork of the Sorgue Valley below, silver with olive trees, and purple with grapes ready to be harvested. The church is just a few steps from our door.

At the very top of the village is a twelfth-century château where the Marquis de Sade, the literary pornographer and advocate of the no-pain, no-gain school of sexual intercourse, spent his childhood inventing sadism. He probably started small, by pulling the wings off flies. He would spend his adult years, when he wasn't in jail or an insane asylum, loving it up in a castle in nearby Lacoste.

The only commercial enterprise in town is a bistro, Lou Clapas. At first, we figure the bistro was named after someone named Lou Clapas. Then, as we become more familiar with the area, we notice a number of restaurants named Lou Something or Other, causing us to deduce that all of these Lous comprised a chain of restaurants, like Howard Johnson, owned by a guy named Lou. Days after we'd gotten comfortable with that explanation, we find that *Lou,* in the ancient Provençal language called langue d'Oc, means "the," and *clapas* means "stone."

We notice, too, as we drive around, that the signs designating town names appear first in contemporary French with the ancient Provençal name printed just below. There is a concerted effort, at least in the Vaucluse, the region in which we will rent for four consecutive years, to preserve the Provençal language. Vaucluse means "closed valley" or Vau-Cluso, and closed it is, surrounded by various mountain ranges, including the highest peak in the Luberon range, Le Mont Ventoux, windy mountain. A storm in the Vaucluse, we will soon find out, is a tympanic thrill as the thunder, trapped in the valley, bounces repeatedly off the valley walls, unable to escape.

The region is also bounded by two of France's greatest rivers, the Durance and the Sorgue. The Sorgue is fed by runoff from Le Mont Ventoux, which, after traveling through a network of underground caves, bursts forth into a huge cavern in what will become one of our favorite towns, Fontaine de Vaucluse, once called La Fònt de Vauclusa.

Buddhism is still looking good, until we attempt to get my computer and Larry's cell phone to work. No matter what house we rent in the future, no matter how much adaptive technology we bring with us, no matter how strongly our landlords assure us that we will have no problems getting online, we can't. It's *il ne marche pas* over and over again, ensuring that we will spend too much of our first three days in any house dwelling in a digital dystopia. Plugging into another country's electrical current is such a challenge that it makes us wish we were home, but neither of us dares say so out loud.

We have neighbors across our narrow street, the Rogets. They introduce themselves. René and Danielle are a retired couple. In French, the condition of being retired is *à la retraite*, which translates literally as "in retreat," as if one were a soldier in a defeated army. Is that better or worse, I wonder, than American retirement, which suggests it's time to go to bed.

He was a banker; she the director of a girls' school. They invite us into their home for an introductory drink. I had thought the French were unfriendly and rarely invited foreigners into their homes, but that is not the case in Provence, as we will continue to learn.

The dominant feature in the living room is a full-color, life-sized, acrylic sculpture of Louis Armstrong. René explains in slow, easy French, enhanced by gestures, that he was eleven years old, living in Paris, when the Americans liberated the city. They gave him *du chocolat* and introduced him to *le jazz*.

4

He loves Americans. During the month, they will invite us for cocktails and take us to an American movie, *Man of La Mancha*. The subtitles are in French. We are at first surprised, but then delighted, to learn that there are no movie theatres in Saumane, nor, for that matter, in L'Isle sur la Sorgue. Nothing is coming to a multiplex near you. It's coming to a grange in the nearby town of St. Didier.

The grange is a modern building, located on a side street where tourists never go. There we are, helping our neighbors set up the folding chairs and putting them away at the end of the show. We chat with them and munch on cookies. Danielle and René introduce us to their friends.

"You have only been studying for two weeks and you speak so well?" they say, and we smile sweetly, forgetting to mention our three years of high school French. One of them will invite us, along with René and Danielle, to her house the next day for an aperitif. Meeting one's neighbors is an important component of belonging. Tourists don't have neighbors.

We meet more neighbors during our stay in Saumane by attending La Fête de la Musique, a potluck event to which Larry contributes a dish. The music is recorded. Yves, Catherine's partner, is the emcee, playing records over a loud speaker. He introduces us to some of the villagers. Larry is determined to knock their Provençal socks off by making mac and cheese. He has thoughtfully modified this dish for French palates by using gruyère instead of cheddar. He explains in his best French to the housewives who are serving up their coq au vin, *tartes aux tomates,* or *quiches lorraines,* that his dish is called "mac and cheese" and that it is uniquely American. He repeats its name slowly, carefully, like a teacher—"mac and cheese." They smile, taste it, and tell him how much they enjoy it. In the fullness of time, we will find out that mac and cheese, made with gruyère, is an authentically French dish, a regular offering on pretty nearly every bistro menu in Provence.

TOTALLY IMMERSED

Our lives in Saumane are organized around our French lessons. The need to understand and be understood is critical to any pretense at Frenchiness. One of my great regrets is that I didn't take my junior year abroad in France. As a result, I am now trying to learn a foreign language at the same time that I am forgetting words in my native tongue. Still, we must work with what neurons are left. It's probably a losing game, but we figure it's *how* we play the game that counts.

We have been lucky with Catherine, and we are lucky with Monique, who we quickly learn to call "Mo." She, even more than the house and the sweet town of Saumane, makes this experience better than anything we might have dreamed. This may be the first time that one of my fantasies turns out as well as I've imagined. I suppose that is bound to happen every once in a while.

She is a superb French teacher, animated, humorous, intelligent, artistically talented, disciplined, and inventive. Sometimes we study grammar per se, attempting to drill verb declensions into our heads. More often, we learn grammar, vocabulary, and French culture by singing songs, listening to tapes, watching films, cooking meals, and taking field trips.

In class, we are totally immersed, as promised. English never crosses our lips. When we don't understand the meaning of a French word, Mo explains it by using other French words. When we can't find *le mot juste* to say precisely what we think or feel, we settle for some circumlocution that we hope gets to the heart of the matter. The air fairly buzzes with the strain of trying. I enjoy the effort, although failure always lurks. I often launch myself into the conversation with only the vaguest idea of what I'm going to say or how I'm going to say it, a sense of dread that sailors in medieval times must have experienced when they approached the place on the map that read, "Beyond here there be dragons." Because there are so many words I do not know, I am obliged to beat around the verbal bush. The unknown noun for interview, *entretien*, becomes "a meeting where you ask people questions and they answer." I am by nature longwinded. At home it's because I think out loud and like to hear myself talk. Here it's because I'm stalling, searching for words.

I love words, all words, written or spoken. One of my earliest childhood memories is my delight in learning "cat," the first word I could spell and read. I must have been in first grade. I ran all the way home that day, spelling and saying "C-A-T cat,

C-A-T cat" over and over again to myself, as if I held the word in a saucer and the letters might spill out and be lost. "C-A-T cat!" I cried as I burst through the kitchen door in search of my mother, eager to present her with my prize.

Each word I learn in Mo's class is a little treasure I add to my trove. The French language is as beautiful and subtle as it is difficult to learn. All French parts of speech are annoying for one reason or another, verbs especially. If they don't feel like acting rational, they don't. If they prefer to be indirect and subtle, they are. Take the verb *manquer*, which means "to miss" or "to lack." You'd think that if you wanted to say, as we so sensibly do in English, "I miss you," you'd say, *"Je manque vous."* But no, that would be too straightforward. Well, then, what about *"Je vous manque."* I you miss, now that we've learned that the pronoun always precedes the verb in the French language? You'd still be wrong. The French would have you say, *"Vous me manquez,"* you are missing to me. And don't even get me started on the subjunctive. Of course English is at least as difficult to learn as French, but you're missing the point. I'm not trying to be fair. I'm trying to be French.

Larry and I have different speaking styles in class. I talk a lot. I'm a glutton for attention. When Larry is finally able to get a word in edgewise, he shows himself to be very strong on nouns and verbs but weak on all other parts of speech. And sometimes his efforts to roll the French letter *r* bring on fits of glottal stoppage. As a result, he speaks like a French Hemingway, very spare and muscular. Whatever words he doesn't know he simply leaves out, and you get to fill them in and make sense of it all.

I prefer to talk rather than to listen, another flaw I've imported from my real life, which is undoubtedly why I, more often than Larry who does listen, do not understand what Mo is saying. Since I'm not fond of humiliation, when I don't understand what's being said, I sometimes fake it. Usually this happens near the end of the classroom day when I'm as overstuffed as a goose's liver. I affect a fixed, interested smile, not too wide in case she's talking about a murdered loved one, and I nod but not too vigorously, hoping that she won't ask any questions that will betray my deception. I worry that she may detect the absence of intelligent light in my eyes. Perhaps she can smell my fear.

Sort of but not quite understanding is just as perilous. I pick up a word or two. I think I get the gist. Somebody is building something very large, something *très grand* in her backyard. I fairly vibrate with frustration. A very large what? It's like standing on tiptoe, trying to pick a delicious, ripe pear that hangs just a millimeter out of reach. When I actually *do* understand, I tend to get extravagantly animated. My eyes sparkle, as if Mo were saying the most exciting things to me. Now I'm not faking. To me, merely understanding is a very big deal. I cry out "*d'accord*," I understand, or "*tout à fait*," absolutely! I hang on her every word.

Mo is determined that we should learn to tell time in the traditional French twenty-four-hour system, this in spite of the fact that lots of French people will make a dinner date for *sept heures*, seven o'clock, instead of *dix-neuf heures*, nineteen hours. No matter how hard I try, I rarely get it right, which is why René and Danielle show up at nineteen hours, my time 7:00 p.m., an hour early for our cocktail party. I had meant to invite them for twenty hours, eight o'clock my time. They sit stiffly in the salon while I rush about preparing hors d'oeuvres and apologizing for getting the time wrong. *"Je suis désolée,"* I tell them. "I'm sorry." (One adds an extra *e* if the speaker is feminine and an *s* if two or more people are *désolés,* or a double *e* and one *s, désolées,* if the speakers are both feminine. Even French adjectives are sex-driven.)

"Désolé" to my ears seems an overly dramatic way to say you're sorry for getting the time wrong. "My best friend is dying." That's *désolé*. And then there's *merde*, which sometimes means "shit" and at other times means "good luck." Go figure.

There are many more French utterances that seem over the top to native English speakers. For instance, I stifle a giggle every time I ask directions from a stranger. Mo has taught us to say, *"Excusez-moi de vous déranger,"* literally, "Excuse me for deranging you," as if the person might otherwise go bonkers. When introduced to someone, it is proper to shake that person's hand and say *"Enchanté de faire votre connaissance,"* or just plain *"enchanté."* Maybe I really am happy to meet you, but enchanted? It also seems to me that *"Je t'embrasse,"* I kiss you, is a bit of a bodice ripper of a sign-off at the end of a letter, when all you really mean is "Love." But, hey, they're French.

When it comes to numbers, I'm in deep trouble. The left side of my brain, the side that's thought to be in charge of numbers, is the size of a garbanzo bean. On the college math aptitude tests, I scored 30 percent of a possible 100. I add on my fingers. If I can, I secrete them under a table and count by pressing them on my knees. I also can't program the TV or balance my checkbook. This is not because I am lazy, or rather not merely because I'm lazy. It is also because I am hardwired numerically hopeless. If, God forbid, Larry should predecease me, I would have to move to assisted living in order to watch Netflix.

Larry has no difficulty with numbers. When he's bored on the road, he adds and multiplies the numbers on license plates, which makes him very adept at dealing with the way the French count. I have no trouble counting to twenty in French, since there's a single word for each number. But once past twenty, or *vingt*, all hell breaks loose. Twenty-one is *vingt et un*, twenty plus one. The seventeenth century is *le dix-septième siècle*, or ten plus seven. And it gets worse. If someone is ninety years old, he "has" *quatre-vingt-dix ans*. That's four times twenty plus ten. And that's not all the "haves" you have to worry about. One isn't hungry, thirsty, or cold; one has hunger, thirst, and cold. But the weather doesn't have hot; it *makes* hot.

And why does every article that precedes every noun have to be either masculine "le" or feminine "la"? I complain to Monique. Why couldn't they settle for a simple "the" like normal Americans? It's not as if *le* or *la* make any sense. One might conclude that the French are oversexualized. The word for magnet is the same as the word for loving, *aimant*, but when it comes to gender, they are merely bewildering. The word for vagina is *le vagin*, and it's masculine. The coarse word for penis is *la bite*, and it's feminine. The word for garbage can, *la poubelle*, is so lovely that I want to dab some behind my ears.

Larry and I like to pit masculine words against feminine words to determine which gender wins the moral high ground. Peace, *la paix*, is feminine, I submit, but so, counters Larry, is war, *la guerre*. Yes, that's true, I allow, but *la vie*, life, is feminine, but so, says Larry, is death, *la mort*. Fed up, Monique has to separate us like the class clowns we are and explain that the le-ness and la-ness of French derives from ancient Latin and would we please stop wasting time.

TALKING FRENCH WITH YOUR MOUTH FULL

At noon, after two hours of French grammar cum culture, Larry and I go downstairs to Mo's dining room where Ange joins us.

Mo sets a pretty table, with tablecloth and matching napkins. The first course, what we would call the appetizer, the French call the *entrée* which in this case consists of *pâtés* and sausages accompanied by the ever-present baguette. Then she serves a *soupe au pistou* a vegetable and bean soup resembling minestrone but seasoned with a mixture of basil, parmesan cheese, and garlic. Just when I think that's got to be it, Mo presents *le plat*, the main course, a brined pork served with her own onion jam. That is followed by the requisite green salad and a cheese plate.

In the South of France, we learn, they eat their major meal at noon. That way they can eat and drink themselves into a stupor, just in time for their siesta, which starts at around two o'clock and goes on until about four. Eyelids and shop doors close for at least two hours.

Without being aware of it, we have been drinking a mild Provençal rosé throughout the meal, and we're pleasantly looped. In *vino* we find not *veritas* but a *soupçon* of uninhibited fluency. Lunchtime conversation chez Mo—at Mo's house— while sometimes incomprehensible, is never boring. However, to stand a chance of participating, we must remain in a state of heightened awareness. Ange, we learn, is Corsican, which is why this household is so well supplied with *figatelli*, a Corsican sausage that tastes like Genoa salami but chewier and more gamey. He is a retired naval engineer and helixophile, someone who collects and sells antique corkscrews, a popular hobby in France. Ange displays his collection at a booth in the antiques section of the Sunday market in L'Isle sur la Sorgue. Occasionally he sells one.

Ange tells us that there's a corkscrew museum in Mènerbes, another pretty nearby hill town. We decide to go. The corkscrews are all just corkscrews at the operative end, but each of the more than thousand handles are different—a dog, a sailboat, a pencil, a crescent moon, a rainbow, a pig, a cart, a hat, a wine bottle, and, our favorite, a naked man with his legs spread wide. There's a bottle cap museum near our home, but in forty years it has never occurred to us to go. Here, out of place, devoid of our usual cynicism—a corkscrew museum? Let's go! We're up for anything. We like ourselves better this way.

Mo and Ange seem genuinely sad and hurt by how anti-French so many Americans seem to be because the French oppose the war in Iraq. The French we know are very well versed on American politics. They are bewildered that the US Congress has recommended that the french fries served in the cafeteria be listed on the menu as "Freedom Fries." (Never mind that so-called french fries actually originated in Belgium.) The French, say Monique and Ange, love Americans even when they dislike our political leaders. Why then, they ask, can't Americans disagree with their government and still love them? They seize upon us as exceptions. Inadvertently we find ourselves cast in the role of ambassadors of good will from a country of ill will.

Both Larry and I are surprised by how much the French people we meet know about America and about their own culture. Our sample is small, but that doesn't keep us from leaping to conclusions. Monique, Ange, and others we will meet at *chez Mo* may or may not be college graduates, but they seem to know as much or more about our culture than we do, and a great deal more about France than most Americans know about America. The first may be due to the high quality of France's public education; the second to the worldwide dominance of American culture.

We laugh a lot and tell stories about children and grandchildren, likes and dislikes, our friends, their friends, the pros and cons of dog ownership, what we did yesterday after school, and whether or not we should buy a French Scrabble set (too many e's). Many of our conversations are political. Mo and Ange are liberals who are horrified, as are we, by our doctrine of preemptive wars, our country's increasing conservatism, and failure to properly separate church and state. We discuss the differences between our legal and educational systems. Other big topics, upon which we agree, are the shameful rise of French anti-Semitism, terrorism, and the increasing hostility toward the peaceful Muslim citizens in their midst.

A particular lunchtime conversation starkly contrasts French and American attitudes toward marriage. Is the idea of commitment learned or felt? Mo wonders. But what Mo and Ange, both of whom have been divorced, find laughable is the whole concept of "for better or for worse, until death do us part."

"Why suffer?" they ask. What's the point? And they practice what they preach. Ange will soon be replaced by Marc, and Mo by another woman. And it won't stop there. Before we leave Provence for the fourth time, Monique will have gone through three lovers, and Ange will be in Canada living out of wedlock with his first wife.

And why bother to marry at all? We Americans, they say, are too earnest in our attitudes toward marriage. I am so eager to be French that I find myself questioning my fidelity. Why *did* Larry and I marry? And why haven't we split up? God knows those thoughts have occurred to us both. We've stuck it out through plenty of "worse." What *was* the point anyway?

For the moment, I seem to have forgotten that I am not French. Part of immersing oneself in a foreign culture can be a temporary loss of one's moral compass. To prove I'm not a hopeless bourgeois, I tell them about my late, free-spirited aunt Lily who had five husbands and didn't waste any time in between. Lily practiced what she called "serial monotony." As soon as one husband lost his allure, she'd move on to another. Mo and Ange express their admiration, but they fault her for bothering to get married, especially after the first time.

It is at Mo's table that we first meet her good friends Sylvie and Alain Prétot. Sylvie is a dark-haired, lively, bright-eyed charmer, a proud housewife and mother of two teenage daughters. Alain, a tall, sturdy fireman by trade, sports an impressively full, long, black, Provençal handlebar moustache that reaches to his jaw line and encloses the lower part of his face in bold parentheses.

He speaks French with a twangy, Provençal accent. The difference between the Parisian accent we study with Mo and Alain's is as distinct as clipped New England speech is to an Alabama drawl. For instance, the way to say "tomorrow morning" is *demain matin*, pronounced "deh-meh meh-teh." Alain pronounces it "demang matang." He speaks slowly. I find his accented French easy to understand. His manner is gentle, even courtly. I develop a crush on him. He speaks no English. I hardly know him. I don't need to know him. He is my fantasy man, the living embodiment of ancient Provence.

Alain, who is deeply devoted to his Provençal heritage, is the first contemporary person anywhere to make the long, narrow barque-like fishing boats called *les nego-chin,* pronounced "lay nay-go-sheen." Extrapolated from langue d'Oc, it means boats so skinny and shallow that even a dog standing in the widest part, the middle of such a boat, is likely to fall into the Sorgue and drown. *Chien* is the modern word for dog. *Noyer,* to drown, is the modern infinitive for *nego.* Alain tells us that during the Middle Ages, when the pope was in Avignon, fishermen wielding implements similar to Neptune's trident, speared trout each Friday and delivered them in *les nego-chin,* and then, when the river narrowed, by cart to Avignon as a tribute to His Holiness.

Alain has made almost 150 of these boats so far. They are his passion. After lunch one afternoon, Alain invites us into his world. He shows us his workshop. He demonstrates his age-old chiseling technique.

Would we like to go for a ride? We walk a couple of blocks toward the center of town, where he keeps his boats tied on the banks of the Sorgue. Larry and I go on separate trips. Three people in a nego-chin is asking for trouble. Alain stands in the back of the boat, propelling it forward with a pole, like a Venetian gondolier, while each of us scooch down on all fours, like a nego-chin.

That first season we also meet Ellen Grenniesen, an American transplant in Provence and one of Mo's former students, who occasionally joins Mo's table to visit and to get a French language booster shot.

She makes her first appearance at the end of a lunchtime conversation class. It has been what I call one of my dreaded "days of malediction." I can't put a French sentence together. Mo likes to joke that *mon cerveau est en panne*, that my brain has broken down, the same phrase they use to describe a car that won't start.

Ellen is married to Bob, the European representative of Back Roads International. Along with their three young children, they have been stationed in Provence for almost two years. Bob, because he deals mostly with Americans, has managed to avoid fluency, but Ellen has seized the opportunity to go native, to integrate herself into the Provençal culture with élan. She trades English lessons for French cooking lessons with her next-door neighbor. She tried to raise chickens in her backyard. The foxes literally raided the hen house, putting an end to that earnest effort, but her vegetable garden thrives. She now speaks French well enough to serve on the PTA of her daughter's school, where wine is served at the meetings. I am charmed by the fact that as her children outgrow their shoes, she fills them with dirt, plants flowers in them, and lines them up on the stone wall in front of her house.

We go on hikes with Ellen and Bob who are so well integrated into *la vie* Provençale that they know the territory and its hidden delights. We are their tourists. When we're with the Greeneissens, we don't have to pretend we're French; we just have to pretend we're young.

On one of our frequent hikes, we follow their lead on what must be at least a three-mile-long, uphill trail through the woods to a restaurant *biologique* called La Pause. How so specialized a restaurant can sustain itself in the woods, so far from anywhere, amazes me. When we arrive, I need more than the pause that refreshes. I need a massage, a nap, and a performance-enhancing IV drip.

As we are eating our biologically correct crêpes and salads at the outdoor picnic table, the owner comments on how the children have grown since their last visit. *"Ils poussent comme des mauvaises herbes."* They're growing like weeds.

After lunch, Ellen has something else she wants to show us, an abandoned hamlet called Barbaranque. Amidst the cluster of tumbled-down stone houses and underbrush, we find a plaque to the memory of its citizens who were massacred on that very spot by the Nazis during the Second World War, a grim reminder that Provence is not all sunlight and lavender.

On the way down, trailed by a gang of goats, we pass the two-story troglodyte dwelling, carved into a cliff, where the local goatherd and his wife live; the goats on the first floor, the couple on the second. Ellen's been trying to get the goatherd to teach her how to make goat cheese. She's been phoning him for days, but he hasn't returned her calls. In spite of its primitive appearance, his cave is equipped with a phone and a fax.

NEVER TRY TO ACT OUT "SAUSAGE" IN A SUPERMARKET

Our first attempt to figure out a French supermarket is a disaster of confusion. No matter how hard we tug at the last cart in the cart corral, we can't get it loose. Then we realize that, as in an airport, one must insert a euro into a slot in order to release a cart. French women still push supermarket carts, but even more of them come equipped from home with large canvas bags on casters, which skip the middleman by serving as both cart and bag.

Once inside, Larry, food lover extraordinaire, slips behind the linguistic barricades and morphs into commander in chief of all that's purveyed.

Larry thinks of supermarkets, whether French or American, as food museums, or maybe libraries. He loves to read the shelves. He's especially excited by the display of fruit juices. "Jus d'orange, jus de poire, jus d'abricot," he exclaims and puts one of each in his wagon. He can spend two hours fully engaged in a supermarket doing research, or merely marveling that the French sell *bouillabaisse* in vacuum-sealed glass jars and *foie gras* in the meat department.

Supermarkets overwhelm me by their size and the variety of goods they offer. They make me feel stupid. First of all, the same side of my brain that struggles with numbers handicaps me when it comes to spatial relations. I have trouble finding my way through the aisles of my local Super Stop and Shop. It's way too super. I encounter a profusion of green leafiness: romaine, mâche, radicchio, frisée, Boston, bib, kale, arugula, spinach, baby and grown-up, in addition to mixes of all of the above. I remember when lettuce was iceberg. I have the same problem in the shampoo department. I yearn for the days when mustard was a matter of Dijon or French's, and shampoo was either Breck or Prell.

Now imagine me trying to navigate a strange supermarket in France where not only must I locate each item, I must translate it. It takes me fifteen minutes to find the milk and another two to figure out that *écrémé* means skimmed.

If I hadn't run into our neighbor René, I never would have found the garbage bags. I didn't know the French word for garbage at the time, *les ordures*, so I shifted into charade mode and acted out a garbage man carrying a heavy bag over his shoulder.

At first René looked perplexed, he must have thought I was doing Père Noël, Santa Claus, but then his eyes lit up in recognition, and he led me over to *les sacs à ordures*.

I make my way to the cereal aisle. I know the word, *les céréales*, but I face yet another stupefying challenge. I'm looking for bran flakes, but I haven't any idea of how to say it, so it wouldn't make any sense to launch into my "excuse me for deranging you" routine.

Trying to settle down in another country is not for everyone. Feeling disoriented and stupid on a daily basis is not everyone's *verre de vin.* Neither is losing your way, or the embarrassment you feel when you carefully look up all the French words you need to ask someone for directions to the pharmacy, *"Où est la pharmacie?"* only to realize that there's *pas une chance* that you will understand the answer.

To make matters worse, I am unfamiliar with French brand names. I look at the pictures on the packages but cannot tell the difference between one kind of flake and another. When at last I find Kellogg's All Bran amidst the alien Corn Chex, I hug the box as if it were a long-lost friend.

The produce department presents a puzzling challenge. Some of the fruits and vegetables are displayed loosely in bins, much as they are in my supermarket at home. Others are segregated in slatted wooden crates, labeled with their country of origin, often Spain, but sometimes other countries, including England and Belgium. I learn later that this produce segregation is the indirect result of a food fight of a complaint brought by the Commissioner of European Communities in 1997 against the French Republic, for failing to take "all necessary and proportionate measures in order to prevent the free movement of fruit and vegetables as required by treaty." It seems that French farmers had been massing at the borders of Spain and Belgium, sometimes destroying or otherwise preventing lorries full of fruits and vegetables from entering their country. As a result, foods must now be labeled with their country of origin. I assume the unlabeled produce comes from France, and so, being French myself, I select what I want from the bins.

Meanwhile, over near the meat counter, Larry's sausage imitation is drawing a crowd. "Just point!" I cry desperately, turning his attention to the phalanx of sausages lined up in the glass display case. Larry has no trouble choosing. He chooses them all. Then he moves on to breads. While I worry about which one is best, Larry takes four and tosses them in his cart, which already contains the juices, organ meats from assorted animals, hard, soft, and semisoft cheeses from cows and goats, and a variety of regional red wines.

Checking out is a nightmare of incomprehension: we should have weighed certain items before showing up at the cashier's line. You can't separate the bananas the way you can at home. You have to pay for the plastic bags. I barely understand a word the checkout lady is saying to us. My eyes well up with tears of humiliation and frustration. Larry, who can't wait to cook up a pituitary gland or two, is in high spirits. He sorts his way through our ineptitude and pays the bill, 150 euros. When we return our cart, the slot spits out a euro.

Once home, we carry the bags of groceries from the street into the house. Here, because our street is so narrow that no other car can get past ours, we are obliged to unload the groceries as fast as we can. That done, one of us drives forward to the square, turns around, drives past our house to the church parking lot, and walks home. How wonderfully inconvenient! How French! Ditto for the garbage. Since no truck can enter the village, we must walk the bags partway down the hill to the green bins.

While unpacking Larry's juice collection into our refrigerator, I break one of the glass shelves. If that happened at home, I'd mutter an expletive, pick up the phone, and call the local glass repair store. In Saumane, a minor disaster presents both a challenge and, depending on your mood, an opportunity. Larry reaches for the French-English dictionary to find the French word for shelf. It could be *l'étagère* or *le rayon*. We decide to go with *rayon*, since the only étagère we know of was in Larry's mother's living room and held books and bric-a-brac. We look up "glass"; it's *la vitrine*. In the yellow pages we find *un vitrier*, which is what they call a guy who deals with glass. Then we play rock-scissors-paper to determine which one of us will be unlucky enough to have to dial the number and speak French to whoever answers. And then, of course, we have to find the place.

Cooking and Eating Provence

Larry was born with silver taste buds in his mouth. Just as Yo-Yo Ma at a very young age could accept nothing less than Pablo Casals for his musical mentor, and covered his ears when his mother played Montavani, so little Larry's inner gourmet complained of stomachaches when confronted by his mother's cooking.

Larry's mother believed that food was necessary but dangerous. To render it harmless, food should be submerged in boiling water until it gave up and turned gray, after which it is best buried under cream of mushroom soup. The only exception was chicken or fowl. He will eat duck but only if it's crispy. Birds should be sautéed quickly until medium rare, which is why Larry doesn't eat chicken or even turkey. On Thanksgiving, he makes himself an omelet.

Larry didn't want to hurt his mother's feelings, so at meal times he faked stomachaches. Eventually, his concerned parents sent him to the hospital for tests, where he drank barium and endured all manner of probes and other intestinal indignities. Like the stoic Spartan boy who stole a fox and hid it under his cape, allowing the fox to eat into his stomach rather than confess to stealing, loyal Larry suffered rather than confess to being revolted by his mother's cooking. His ordeal did not end until he went away to college and encountered what at first he thought was gourmet cooking. Then he married me and learned better.

"I don't eat anything that flies," he warned me when we got engaged. For a while he was satisfied to be out of pain and bird-free. I cooked all-American recipes from *Fanny Farmer* and Irma Rombauer's *The Joy of Cooking*.

Then, in the 1980s, Julia Child introduced Americans to French cooking. Larry sat up and took notice. Her recipe for French bread filled eleven pages. It required that Larry rise at three in the morning in order to pound the dough down for its third and final rise and then insert a steaming brick into the oven to ensure that the bread came out varnished, like a Strad.

Ever since Julia, Larry's been reading cookbooks for fun. He is not discouraged by complex recipes. I, by contrast, read them to find fast and easy meals. One half hour of preparation time is my limit. I skip over recipes that begin, "The day before, peel and poach 12 plover's eggs," or include words like cheesecloth, blanche, reduce, knead, whisk, parchment paper, or nasturtium petals. I am attracted to those that have no more than eight ingredients, including salt and pepper. I also avoid recipes that require one to soak anything overnight in favor of those that begin with the reassuring words, "Preheat oven to 350 degrees." We are a culinary odd couple, worse than Jack Sprat and his wife.

Now that we're in Provence, Larry prefers cookbooks written in French to comprehensible ones in English, although English versions are readily available in the bookstore in the center of L'Isle sur la Sorgue. As a result, Larry needs a dictionary to translate some of the ingredients, and a table of equivalences, which French cookbooks don't provide, to decipher the measurements.

"Is a *litre* more or less than a quart?" he wonders, tossing a few cups of water into the pot. Larry can be very careless about amounts. He tends to double the garlic. He can also be pretty devil-may-care about ingredients. He used to think that Worcestershire sauce and anchovies enhanced pretty nearly every recipe with the exception of Toll House cookies. In that respect, I am also his opposite: I follow directions like a fascist.

Occasionally I cook. I have noticed that tomato pie is the sine qua non of Provençal fare, or at least in September when there are a lot of tomatoes around. We've gone to a few *petite soirees,* and someone invariably brings a tomato pie. It is clear that I cannot even pretend to be a French woman unless I can make *une tarte aux tomates.*

What stops me from trying is that I have never made a successful crust. I do exactly what the recipe says about ice cubes and butter, but I end up with a large lump that looks like a brain and crumbles like plaster. Imagine my delight when I mention my fear of pastry to Monique, and she tells me that it's easy, any *"femme stupide"* can do it. Real French women, she says, no longer make crusts from scratch; they unroll them from Pillsbury. *Sic transit gloria mundi.*

For the most part, the recipe conforms to my culinary prerequisites: not too many ingredients; degree of difficulty, one; degrees of temperature, around 400 degrees F. Our oven is French, so I must twist the knob to the approximate French equivalent, which Larry estimates is 200 degrees C.

Tarte aux Tomates
(makes an 8- to 9-inch pie)

Ingredients

Pillsbury or other prepared pie crust
3 large tomatoes, cut into half-inch slices salt
1 pound gruyère cheese, cut into thin slices
1 teaspoon dried basil or 1 tablespoon finely cut fresh basil
freshly ground black pepper
3 tablespoons grated parmesan cheese

Prebaking the Pastry—The Hard Part

Rub butter on the bottom and sides of a cake pan or quiche pan that's no more than 1 1/4 inches deep.

Unroll cold pastry and lower it carefully and evenly into the pan, pressing the pastry into the bottom and sides of the pan. Cut off excess pastry with a knife or scissors. Use a fork to prick the bottom of the pastry, but don't prick it all the way through.

Preheat oven to 400 degrees F. The pricks won't be enough to keep the pastry from bubbling, so butter a piece of aluminum foil and press it, buttered side down, on the bottom and side of the pastry. Bake in the middle of the oven for 10 minutes, take out of the oven, and remove the foil. Then prick the pastry again (again, not all the way through) and return it to the oven for three minutes or until the pastry is slightly browned and has begun to pull away from the sides of the pan. Remove from oven and cool.

Directions for Filling—The Easy Part

Sprinkle the tomato slices with lots of salt and place them on a cake rack to drain for about half hour, or if you don't have a cake rack, use paper towels.

Arrange cheese slices, slightly overlapping, on the bottom of the pastry shell. Place the drained tomato slices side by side on top of the cheese. Sprinkle a couple of grindings of black pepper, the basil, and the parmesan on top. Bake in the upper third of the oven for 25 minutes, or until the cheese has melted and the edges of the pie are nicely browned.

The tomatoes need too much time to drain, and there's a bit too much pricking of the crust with a fork, but I obey my way through it. The tomato pie becomes my specialty, my calling card, not so much for its quality, it's pretty hard to screw up, but because I rarely cook anything else. If we stayed longer than a month, they'd find me out. "Oh here comes Mary-Lou again with her tomato pie."

THE STUFF CENTER OF THE WORLD

Tourists don't visit supermarkets, but they, along with the native Provençaux flock to the weekly outdoor markets for which Provence is well known, and so do we. Part flea market, part food market, part circus, part social gathering place, and part country fair, the markets are the most defining aspect of traditional Provençal life.

At the outdoor markets, some French women still carry genuine French *paniers*, straw shopping baskets with leather handles, although small white recyclable plastic bags are taking over. In ecologically sensitive American towns where plastic bags are also no longer available from merchants, French *paniers* are getting a handhold, at least among the pretentious.

The atmosphere among vendors and customers alike is festive and friendly. Even as the vendors hustle by offering potential customers free samples of cheeses and sausages, they pause to chat. The goods are displayed attractively in pottery bowls and baskets, on makeshift tables and in stalls: a giant, carbon steel pan of paella looks like a still life. Prices are written in pencil or ink on cut-out squares of cardboard, or in chalk on small framed slates, the kind French children carry to school. Or at least it pleases me to think they still do. What makes the markets especially authentic and appealing is that customers are waited on by the very farmers who have grown the food they're selling.

Inevitably, modernity has inserted itself into the traditional weekly markets. An amplified rock band sets up in front of the charcuterie. In another part of the marketplace, a woman in peasant clothing cranks out "Under the Bridges of Paris" on her hurdy-gurdy. One has the sense she's been cranking away anachronistically for years.

Markets take place on a fixed day in every village and town throughout Provence. If it's Monday, it's Cadenet; on Tuesday, it's Apt; the big Wednesday market is in St-Rémy-de-Provence; Thursday it's Aix-en-Provence; on Fridays, Lourmarin; and on Saturday, it's Uzes.

Sunday belongs to L'Isle sur la Sorgue, the largest, most copious market in the immediate region. It teems with tourists. My first act is to buy a straw shopping basket into which I cannot wait to add a baguette. When you're pretending to be French, props matter.

We make our way through the slow-moving throng. We are primed to buy by the sheer variety, beauty, and seemingly infinite display. The soaps come in all colors and flavors, including chocolate, good enough to eat. We are drawn to everything: kitchen towels, table linens, lavender sachets, puppies and baby pigs in baskets, African masks, olive wood bowls, bouquets of flowers, honey, and all manner of kitsch variations on the theme of cicadas. In the outdoor markets, this truly bug-eyed bug is as ubiquitous as a horde of grasshoppers to which they are entomologically related. They are everywhere, cicada sachets, doorknockers, lapel pins, salt and pepper shakers, ashtrays, and dish towels. Probably tattoos. Although revered in Provence, in China they eat cicadas. The females are meatier.

The cicada is the celebrity insect of Provence as emblematic in its way as the fleur-de-lis is to the kings of France and the eagle to the United States. The French fabulist La Fontaine, no doubt borrowing from the Greek fabulist Aesop, wrote a fable called *The Grasshopper and the Ant*, although he used the word *cigale* for the grasshopper. In both fables, the cicada is the antihero, a morally reprehensible creature. He hangs out in trees all summer, lazy and carefree, humming a happy tune while the industrious ant spends *his* summer storing away food for winter. In fact, rather than fable, the cicadas are not lounging around and giving voice. They're procreating nonstop. What could be more *louche*, more *insouciant*, more French?

I learn that there are thousands, probably millions of live cicadas hanging out high in the trees above me right now. The male makes a kind of loud noise, which, since male cicadas have no larynx, is produced by rapid retractions of the male's hollow stomach. A female cicada that finds a male attractive will respond to his call by giving her wings a come-hither flick that makes a clicking sound. As the duet continues, the sonar-guided male makes his way toward the female. *Cha*-chi-chi. The accent is always on the first syllable, *cha*-chi-chi, *cha*-chi-chi, *cha*-chi-chi. They go at it all day long. No one in the marketplace seems to notice the perpetual din, although I'm told that if you hold a male cicada up to your ear, his 120-decibel noise—the intensity of a jet engine—can cause permanent hearing loss. Better they should stay in the trees.

Perhaps the natives are so used to the chirring sound that they no longer hear it. But I'm not used to it; I'm just getting to know it. The cicada chorus relaxes me. Their repetitive trill vibrates, filling my brain with a peaceful hum. I suppose, like everything wonderful here, I could accommodate to it and stop hearing their sweet call, too. But please not yet.

In the household appliances section of the market, Larry and I fall under the spell of a fast-talking salesman who is demonstrating a many-bladed vegetable device that curls cucumbers into spirals, sculpts radishes into tulips, and shreds carrots into confetti. We buy one and go home to try it out. It cuts fingers into ribbons. We must restrain each other from trying to acquire all of Provence. We take turns talking each other out of ridiculous purchases. While I'm stroking the patina of an eighteenth-century cobbler's bench and asking the dealer how much it would cost to send it to the United States in a shipping container, it is Larry who knows to deliver the *coup de réalité* by reminding me that we can't afford it, and besides, it wouldn't fit in our kitchen. Similarly, Larry may not buy the clippers that can cut through bamboo. "We don't have any bamboo," I remind him.

We let down our guard when we make our way toward the food. After all, one must eat. We pause to choose among the rows of bright-eyed fish lying gill to gill. We buy gleaming green, brown, and black olives, each color in its own oval basket, each basket supplied with its own long-handled, rough-wooden spoon. We scoop out some of each, dig for coins, and move on to the *pâtes*, sausages, cheeses, fruits, salads, and tiny delicious strawberries—so fresh that unlike their sell-by-date, steroidal American cousins that molder within a day, Provençal berries remain fresh and succulent for at least a week.

The market is a great place to practice our French. Larry is becoming a regular at the *grattons* stand. That's where they sell his favorite food group, grease. Since he can't afford *foie gras*, he'll settle for *grattons*, fried duck skin. He elicits a smile of recognition from the vendor, followed by what has become a ritual exchange.

"*Bonjour,*" says the *gratton* man.

"*Bonjour,*" says Larry. "*Ça va?*"

"*Ça va,*" says the *gratton* man.

"*Une poignée pour messieur?*"

"*S'il vous plaît,*" Larry answers.

The vendor grabs a handful and deposits it into a paper bag.

"*A la prochaine,*" the vendor calls after us. "Until the next time."

"*A la prochaine,*" Larry calls back.

We smile and wave goodbye as if parting from a good friend.

These are the moments we live for; conversations, however trivial, in real-life situations with actual French people who don't know us and might even think we're French, at least for a split second. During the rest of our market stroll, Larry will toss one *gratton* after another into his mouth, as if they were peanut M&Ms. I keep my mouth shut, but I'm thinking, *Quadruple bypass.*

After a month's worth of visits to the market in L'Isle sur la Sorgue, we know our way around. The vendors look familiar to us and we to them. We greet the woman who sells hummus near the *pharmacie.* It is she who explains to me that the word for a plastic container is *une boîte,* an all-purpose French word that means container, can, and box. We recognize the *bouquiniste,* who deals in secondhand French books. We browse there often, looking for written material that we have a chance of understanding. We know who's got the best cheese. We know that the rotisserie chicken that's sold near the church isn't as good as it looks. We even recognize the town weirdo who addresses passersby in Tourette-like blurts, which at first we are unable to translate. Now that we've learned a few more French colloquialisms, we no longer smile sweetly at him when he tells us, "*Va te faire foutre*"—"Go fuck yourselves."

How to Go to the Bathroom

French toilets can be daunting. When I first came to France in the late fifties, most of the toilets were *à la turque*, in the Turkish style. One had to squat on slightly elevated vitreous footprints, hang over a hole while clinging to a rope, and flush by pulling a chain with the other hand, thereby releasing a cataract of water that only the most nimble could outleap. The Turkish toilet is all business, not a facility that invites reading or crossword puzzling.

In spite of the fact that Turkish toilets are outmoded and not user-friendly, there are still plenty of them around, especially in cafes and gas stations, so it is best to be prepared. If you're wearing trousers, squat toilet users recommend pushing the waistline down and rolling your pant legs up to your knees. Skirts are a hazard and are best worn tied around the neck.

There's a perpetual water shortage in this part of Provence in spite of the Durance River, which, along with the Rhône, flows through the valley. Too many people are irrigating vineyards and orchards. Part of the response to this demand for water is the environmentally friendly toilet. Many French toilets come equipped with two circular, shiny steel flushing buttons on the top of the tank, the smaller located inside the larger. The smaller one is calibrated for *pipi* only. These big-flush/little-flush toilets have begun to make their debut in the States.

It should come as no surprise that the French language, as it does in so many situations, makes it as difficult as possible for foreigners to go to the bathroom. "Where is the bathroom?" is what we say in the United States when we're not at home and feel the need to answer nature's call. But if you translate the very same question into French as we did initially—*"Où est la salle de bains?"*—your words will be met with displays of confusion. They'll think you're asking to take a bath.

We don't notice at first, but for Americans, "bathroom" is the euphemism we've inherited for "toilet," although it makes a kind of sense, since, in our country, toilets are usually located in bathrooms. In France, they're not. They're in their own little private room, along with a tiny sink, what we euphemistically call a "powder room." You will get where you want to go if you ask for the internationally accepted term "water closet," or WC. The French don't have the letter W; they just stick two Vs together and voilà, *le double* V. Interesting that we, who also stick two Vs together, call the letter "double U."

Les toilettes is probably the most utilized alternative, but be sure to ask in the plural—*les toilettes*—even though you only need one. Ask for *la toilette* and you risk more confusion, evoking, as you do, the French expression *faire la toilette*. A French woman doesn't simply get dressed. She makes her *"toilette,"* which in this instance has nothing to do with toilets as we know them. The word derives from the word *toile,* which refers to a woven cloth upon which a woman, in earlier times, would lay out her grooming materials, such as her hairbrush, her makeup, and a bottle of *eau de toilette,* which you now know if you didn't before, is not water from the toilet. Only the French could make something sweet smelling out of the word "toilet."

None of the above, however, is good enough for Monique, who has taught us that it is polite to employ a euphemism, *"Je voudrais me laver les mains."* "I would like to wash my hands."

While visiting Sylvie and Alain Prétot, I find myself in need of a toilet. I approach Sylvie and tell her I need to *me laver les mains.* She takes me to the kitchen sink, hands me a fresh dishtowel, and watches while I, temporarily dumbfounded, wash my hands. The flow of water from the faucet leads me to cross my legs in desperation. I blurt out something about a toilet. Sylvie, laughing, leads me to what we would call a powder room, furnished with a toilet and a sink.

When Monique, the linguistic traitor, shows up at the Prétots' for lunch a few minutes later, I call her on it. Not a bit apologetic, Monique shamelessly tells us the story of an American woman who asked the same question at a stranger's house and ended up in a tiny room with only a sink attached to the wall. Too embarrassed to inquire further, the woman made an attempt to mount the sink and—*oh là là*—the sink broke away from the wall and fell to the floor. She collected herself as best she could, exited the bathroom, and explained to the hostess that she had felt faint and grabbed onto the sink, only to have it pull away from the wall.

Finding *les toilettes* when you're out and about is no problem. Contrary to policy in many restaurants and cafes in the States, toilets are not "reserved for customers only." Having been toilet-trained in the United States, it took us awhile to figure out that it is not necessary to sit down and buy something to eat or drink in order to be permitted access to the *les toilettes*. Nor is there any reason to ask to wash your hands. A simple *"Les toilettes?"* does the trick.

Just remember, when back in the States, switch back to the singular. Don't ask to go to the bathrooms.

⊶━╤

HANGING OUT

I develop an unlikely passion in Saumane—hanging out the laundry. I can't get enough of it, in spite of how perilous the journey leading from our back door to the clothesline below. Our house doesn't really have a backyard. After you step onto the lovely stone patio, you face a dramatic falling off of the yard, a virtual cliff into which dozens of rough-cut, suicidal stone steps have been inserted, without aid of banisters. We've noticed that Provençal stairways, both interior and exterior, often lack banisters. Perhaps the French have no building codes, as we do, that require them. Perhaps the French believe that you should take responsibility for yourself, that you should recognize potentially dangerous situations and behave accordingly. Now that I'm French, I agree. "Don't be a klutz," I tell myself as I make my way carefully down the steps, holding a basket full of wet laundry. *"Ne klutzez-vous pas."*

At home, one of my least favorite activities is doing the wash, even though it can hardly be said that I'm doing anything much at all, except switching a load, when I remember, from one Maytag sister to the other. Folding is even worse. But what annoys at home often challenges and delights me here. In Provence, I love doing the wash. I do wash more frequently than necessary, just for the sheer joy of it. Larry thinks I'm crazy, but he raises no protest. While I'm outside hanging, he's inside, stealing a smoke.

Most of the houses in Provence don't have dryers. That's because all of Provence is a dryer. The Provençal sun is so hot and the humidity so low that a pair of blue jeans hanging on the clothesline, with which all houses are equipped, is dry in two hours, even the pockets and waistbands.

The last time I hung out laundry, I was a child. The clothesline was on a pulley, anchored between the exterior wall of the back of our house and a tall tree near the sandbox. I would watch in wonder as my mother, with a single yank, could send the hung wash on its way and make room for what waited in the basket at her feet.

I had the extremely important job of holding the canvas clothespin bag and passing the clothespins to my mother, homemaker extraordinaire, mistress of the mangle, wonder woman of wash. I watched, proud and fascinated, as she'd turn a small bit of the clothing over the line before securing it with a wooden pin. For whatever reason, pin conservation was a goal and part of the ritual. The idea was to use the second pin from one article of clothing, assuming it was an upside-down two-pin shirt, for instance, and not a one-pin sock, to secure one side of the next piece of clothing. I loved the skill and the thrill: the wet sheets billowing, the pleasing order of the final lineup, the humorous appearance of random, dismembered body parts hanging in a ghostly display.

In my backyard in Saumane, it all comes back to me in a Proustian rush. Because the French word for laundry is *le linge*, Larry mocks my nostalgia for *le linge* by calling it *A La Recherche du Linge Perdu*.

But there's more going on here than a madeleine moment. There is pleasure in back-to-basics real work, something I relate to a genuine exploration of another culture. So much physical work is done for us in our real lives at home. Doors swing open. Garage doors lift. Windows rise, and lights turn on automatically. In many public places, water faucets turn themselves on and off. Even toilets flush themselves, terrorizing me at the same time as they invade what I like to think of as my personal space. In Provence, I enjoy the built-in workout that laundry requires. Standing, bending, and reaching in the backyard of my borrowed, old-fashioned world, I find the motions calming, reassuring. There is a meditative quality to the hanging of wash. It takes time. I check it periodically to see how it's doing. And when it's dry, I bury my face in the heady scent of sunshine and grass. Nirvana.

MAKE WAY FOR DUCKS

The night before we are to leave, we give ourselves a farewell dinner party. Ellen recommends that we order take-in from Bernard Chastlelas, the Duck Man. He has a rotisserie truck in nearby St. Didier. He majors in chickens, Ellen explains, but if you call him the night before, he'll prepare his especially delicious olive-stuffed duck. Ellen should know. In addition to every other challenge she has mastered, she's an expert French cook.

The next morning, we set out to claim our ducks. They are not there. M. Chastelas is, of course, *désolé*, but we shouldn't worry. The ducks will be ready at noon.

"What's he planning to do?" says Larry. "Go home and kill them?"

"This is Provence," I defend with the pride of a native. "Maybe they're not done hanging by their feet, or whatever it is they do to ducks."

We had walked through this fifteenth-century town when we went to the movies with the Rogets, but that visit was in the evening, so we never got a good look. Now, under a vividly blue sky, we take a few minutes to enjoy the fact that the main street is lined with century-old plane trees that create an aisle, fine enough for a bride, leading toward an eighteenth-century belfry gate. Larry takes out his camera.

Before we leave, Larry insists upon taking a picture of me with M. Chastelas. I protest. He practically has to drag me to the truck, and then to top it off, Bernard slings an arm around me. One minute I'm like any other Provençal woman buying ducks from an itinerant purveyor, and the next minute my own husband blows my cover.

There's no point in hanging around St. Didier for a couple of hours, so we head back to the supermarket in L'Isle to buy some extra wine and other last-minute items we'll need for the party. We shop with reasonable dispatch. It's taken a month, but I finally know where the eggs are.

We load up the trunk but fail to fully close it. As we drive home to put the purchases in the *frigo*, we hear some strange tinkling noises but figure it's the wine rolling over the potato chips. At another juncture, we hear the same noise and imagine the wine rolling over the eggs that we'd planned to hard-boil. In fact, our groceries are falling out of car and onto the road, but we don't realize this until we get home and find the trunk empty. We retrace our journey. Larry drives. I hang my head out the passenger window, scanning the roadsides for evidences of dinner.

"Ah, yes, there." I point, when we're halfway down the Saumane hill, at our own grocery roadkill—scrambled eggs, blood-red wine, shards of glass, egg shells, and flattened bags of potato chips. We go back to the supermarket and start all over again.

When it's time to return to St. Didier, we decide to go by bike; we've had enough of the car. There's a bit of mistral in the air but not enough to interfere with cycling. It will be our last bike ride, and the weather is perfect. Then we remember the ducks. Larry comes up with a solution. He'll carry them home in his backpack. Once we descend our hill, it's pretty much a flat ride into St. Didier, although too much of it is along a highway. Huge trucks speed by, blowing us sideways with near mistral force, almost sweeping us off our wheels.

Our ducks are ready. Larry discusses this evening's party menu with M. Chastelas, who suggests that we add some white beans to the menu.

"Just heat up the ducks and serve them over the beans. That's the classic Provençal way." He happens to have a few jars in his truck.

It's too bad that we didn't think to bring some plastic bags. M. Chastelas has wrapped the ducks in paper, but that's not going to keep three steaming-hot ducks from exuding whatever ducks exude—grease for sure. I pedal behind Larry all the way home, watching the stain on his backpack expand, take over his T-shirt, and begin to form tiny rivulets that are heading toward his butt.

That night we tape a sign on our door that reads, *"Liberté, Egalité, Amitié."* We mean it, the friendship part especially. Although we hardly know them, Mo, Ange, Sylvie, Alain, Catherine, Yves, René, Danielle, Ellen, and Bob feel like friends.

Between what we have assembled and what the guests have brought, our table is heaped with cheeses, hummus, pâtés, sausages, smoked salmon, a lobster spread, tapenade, and baguettes galore. The French, or at least the French we know, like to make mincemeat out of every animal, vegetable, fish, or bird they can get their hands on. It may be an excuse for eating bread.

Mo brings a tomato pie. Ellen brings a box of Belgian chocolates. René and Danielle, Catherine and Yves, the Prétots and Ange bring wine, which is a good thing because, even though we replaced the broken bottles of wine, we have vastly underestimated how much wine the French will drink. Ange brings his prized antique wooden corkscrew that stands on three legs and looks like a Gatling gun. Yves plays his guitar. We sing. Catherine asks a riddle: Why can't a man be both good-looking and smart? *"Pourquoi?"* ("Why?") We give up. "Because then he'd be a woman."

Our soirée is a great success. The wine and conversation flow freely. It is midnight when we walk Ange and Mo to their car. I, who have the reputation of being about as sentimental as a junkyard dog, burst into tears when it's time to part. We promise each other we'll stay in touch by e-mail. I couldn't bear it if this adieu were not really *à bientôt,* see you soon.

We leave very early the next morning. We slip the keys into Catherine's letterbox and head down the hill for a quick *café* and croissant at Le Café Bellevue, where we encounter Alain on his way to work. We tell him we are *désolés—très très désolés*—to be leaving Provence. He is *désolé* that we are leaving. We exchange warm hugs and triple kisses. *"Il faut partir pour revenir,"* he says, consolingly. You have to leave in order to return.

In the Second Place

The Second Time Around

We love our little house so much that we rent it the following year. Since it's not available for September, we lease it for the last three weeks of June and the first week of July. Coming home turns out to be a mixed blessing. We take great pleasure from the cozy feeling that accompanies returning to rue de L'Eglise. After all, wasn't feeling at home in Provence precisely what we wanted? What better way than to return to the same house, to René and Danielle, to the crazy hill, to Lou Clapas, where we're welcomed back with open arms? And, *grâce à Dieu*, with a bunch of computer adapters that we already know will *marchent*. But here's the rub: repetition exacts a price, novelty.

The first year, we were crazy about the place. If Saumane were a lover, we'd have been locked in a passionate embrace. But we, like all humans, are susceptible to hedonic adaption. Raymond Chandler understood this well when he wrote: "The first kiss is magic. The second is intimate. The third is routine."

We should have known. Passion has a short shelf life. Last year we found it amusing, even delightful, that the faucet in the kitchen sink shot two streams of water straight into our eyes. This time we look up the word for wrench and pay a visit to Monsieur Bricolage, Mr. Do It Yourself, the French equivalent of Home Depot.

Our French has become rusty. I hear our neighbors René and Danielle talking in the street. I don't understand a word they are saying. They might as well be geese honking. Have I forgotten so much French? We've been working so hard to learn this language, and the only person we really understand, at least reliably, is Monique, and that's only because she insists upon it. If something happened to her, we'd only be able to talk incorrectly to one another. Some days we wonder: Will our efforts to learn this language be even more hopeless than the efforts of the proverbial frog—no offense intended—trying to jump out of the well?

Eating at Lou Clapas is also threatening to become routine, as is the once thrillingly tortuous six-kilometer downhill drive to Monique's. And it isn't until this, our second stay, that we realize that Saumane, while a medieval hill town, too closely resembles an American suburb. Everything is a car ride away. For next year, we resolve to rent in a village, where there's plenty of action and commerce.

We also didn't fully appreciate how freaking hot it would be in Provence in June and July. We open the windows, hoping for a premature mistral, and instead get a houseful of flies, *les mouches.*

Our house has no screens. We are told that many people in Provence don't have screens on their windows. Why not? The sun, they say, heats up the screens and ends up adding considerable discomfort to the already impossibly hot afternoons. But so do the flies. Larry adds to the problem by opening the front door as well as the shutters on the windows to get some air, thereby sponsoring a regular *mouche* invitational when what he means to achieve is a mild breeze. *Les mouches* seem to wander in during the day, and then when the air outside begins to cool off—at this time of year at around eight in the evening—they head back outdoors. Even they don't want to be stuck in a hot room full of flies.

Everything changes for the newer and better when another student, Ulrike, "Ulli," joins our classroom. Ulli, sprightly, blond, blue eyed, and pretty, was brought up in East Berlin where her parents were members of a resistance movement that met at the local church. Her partner, Bettina, was raised in the German sector. By contrast, Bettina looks more Indian maiden than *fraulein*, with her long, dark, straight hair and angular good looks. Both of them share the alleged Teutonic qualities of seriousness and discipline, but when they're not devoting themselves to a task, both are humorous and playful.

Ulli and Bettina have left Germany for good and have chosen France as their new homeland. They have recently bought a house in nearby Perrotet, a hamlet that was once a working farm. The outbuildings where wheat, goats, wine, and tools were once housed have been charmingly renovated into dwellings. Ulli and Bettina live in the former lamb shed. That they both speak some English is a decided boon to our friendship.

They seem eager to tell all us their story, and we listen with fascination. They're both in their thirties. Bettina was married in her twenties to a man who understood that she had a preference for women. Apparently he loved her enough, and she him. Moreover, the marriage, which lasted ten years, allowed her to continue to deny her homosexuality.

Ulli has never married, but she dated men exclusively until she met Bettina. Luckily, both sets of parents have come around to appreciate and even love each partner, so now they all feel at ease together. Perhaps they share this information with us right away to test our attitude toward their lesbianism. We, too, feel at ease.

Over this second month, we will spend increasing amounts of time with them. When we do, we always start out speaking French, but when the going gets tough, we ease into English. Bettina already speaks French well and is working at a facility for the handicapped, so she doesn't participate in our class, but Ulli must learn the language quickly in order to find a job. Larry and I are stunned by their courageous move. Their bold commitment reenergizes the meaning of the cliché "making a new life."

Ulli doesn't speak French as well as we do. At last! Someone whose head is lower than mine! I have taken a liking to an all-purpose French phrase, *ça ne fait rien,* which means "it doesn't matter." I drop it carelessly into the conversation whenever it seems to apply. I love it when she turns to me in class and asks me what it means. For one delightful but illegitimate moment, I get to play teacher.

REAL FRIENDS AND FALSE FRIENDS

Larry and I are relieved and encouraged by the fact that many French words—verbs and nouns—are the same in English. Sources differ, but there are between 1,500 and 2,500 such cognates in the French language, and Larry and I grab onto them whenever we get the chance. If one of us wants to ask about someone's reputation—*réputation,* with the accent on the last syllable—it's a good bet. So are *abrasion, abattoir, bandit, bandage, cage, calorie, date, dense,* and hundreds more, right down to *zéro.* We are constantly on the lookout for cognates, or what the French call *vrais amis,* the linguistic equivalent of taking candy from a baby. We hardly ever confess that it's *le même en anglais,* the same in English. We prefer to let Monique think we're well on our way to fluency. What glib fun I have saying that I've eaten too many *calories.*

Meanwhile, Ulli fumes. We have an unfair advantage. The German language offers her no *vrais amis.* On the other hand, Ulli studies like a demon, while we spend only an hour or two a day doing homework, such as memorizing long lists of irregular verbs. We try. We conjugate. We even quiz each other, but our senior brains fight us every *millimètre* of the way. I am more diligent than Larry. I was one of those who spent my grammar school days in the front row trying to get called on, perpetually waving my hand while the teacher scanned the classroom, plaintively asking, "People, must I always see the same hands?"

Now that we're studying French in Provence, I, who spent my lifetime competing for best daughter, best camper, and best student, now compete for best French speaker. Throughout grammar school and high school, my classmates called me a "suck" and a "brown nose." Even in this place, I want to be teacher's pet. I do not, cannot, change my colors in Provence. The little girl in the front row, waving her hand and wanting to be called on, remains alive, well, and obnoxious. Since neither Larry nor Ulli aspire to that calling, I win hands up.

For English speakers, the French language gives with one hand and takes with another. The language takes its revenge by leading one down the primrose path of *les faux amis* where false cognates lurk. French *débutantes* don't come out; a *débutant* is a beginner. *Actuellement*, a particular temptation of mine, means "at the moment," not "actually," and *éditeurs* are publishers, not editors, and a *canape'* is a sofa, and an *etiquette* has nothing to do with manners; it's a label. And while we're at it, it is not a good idea to employ the verb *blesser* if you want to bless someone. You will wound them instead. And then there's the just plain bizarre—neither *faux* nor *vrais*. What do the French call a photographer? *Un photographe*.

Occasionally Mo, very much a free spirit, teaches us words we will never need to know, like the two different words for yeast that are mentioned in an article we read about artisanal bread. Larry doesn't bake bread anymore, and it's been years since I've had a yeast infection.

Life is short. My brain is shrinking; my arteries are filling with plaque. I begin to make a mental list of words to forget. The list lengthens the day Mo hands out three newspaper articles, each one devoted to a different career. Larry gets the one about an *entarteur*, a guy who throws pies in the faces of celebrities. Ulli gets *marinette*, a woman sailor. I get *cascadeuse*, a woman who performs stunts. Larry's and my projected life expectancies are sufficiently brief so that I think we can be confident of never needing either to speak or understand any of them. We need to save the space in our brains for important words like lawyer and writer and heart attack. How perverse, then, that we cannot forget them! *Cascadeuse?* I'm stuck with it. It is seared into my brain. It is branded alongside another useless but unforgettable phrase I learned during my first year of high school French, *vendeur itinérant de peaux de lapin*, an itinerant seller of rabbit skins.

We learn almost as much French when we're out in the streets as we do when we're in a classroom. After examining all the baked goodies on display in our local *pâtisserie*, I point to a particularly good-looking tart, rehearse my request to myself, decide I have it right, and say, *"Je veux cette tarte-là"*—"I want that tart there"—triggering one of what would be many unscheduled but welcome and friendly French lessons from total strangers. The owner explains to me in French that "I want" is too strong and demanding, something a policeman would say. She advises me to say, "*je voudrais*"—"I would like"—instead.

Larry makes his own faux pas, many of them due to minor slips in pronunciation, which, especially in French, can be catastrophic. "*Où est la guerre?*" "Where is the war?" he asks a befuddled Frenchman when he wants directions to the railroad station, *la gare*. Still, he recovers nicely. "*Après moi,*" he jokes, "*le vin rouge.*"

I feel a thrill when I realize that I have finally made a French word or phrase my own. *Tout à fait*, which means "quite," is a very French way of agreeing with someone. So is *d'accord*. "*Ah oui*" is another bit of conversational evidence that indicates that I am understanding, or at least pretending to understand what someone is saying. (Larry, who can sometimes be even more pretentious than I, has noticed that some French people don't pronounce *oui* "wee;" they say "way," so he does too.)

We pick up some basic manners. In Provence, it is proper for the customer to greet the shop owner face-to-face with "*Bonjour, Madame,*" or "*Bonjour, Monsieur.*" At home, it's the opposite; the shopkeeper greets the customer. But in both countries, the goal is to sell.

"*Puis-je vous aider?*" "May I help you?"

"*Je ne fais que regarder.*" "Just looking," I learn to say. "*Merci, nous avons bien mangé,*" I prattle to *maîtres d'hôtels* at the end of a pleasant meal. After lots of practice, thanking the host for having eaten well now flows trippingly off my tongue. We add almost daily to our repertoire of words and phrases. We begin to think in French. This is one of the acknowledged intermediate stages on the way to fluency, one, alas, we will not get far beyond.

Even though we know a lot of words relating to French food, we still have trouble translating some menu offerings. We know that *court bouillon* is fish stock, not the spare change that Louis XIV left on his bureau at Versailles, but what are *blanquettes de gras-double au pistou*? Blankets with extra grass and pistons? Can't be. Or what to make of *cervelles de veau en matelote*? Servile veal in a mattress? Unlikely. *Tête d'Ane farcie* can't be humorous head of donkey. We know that Gallantine and Mousseline are not two of the Three Musketeers, but what are they? I search in vain for my bilingual fail-safe: filet mignon. We take our puny revenge when menus in French are also translated into fractured English, and *pieds et paquets à la Provençale* becomes feet and packages in Provence.

We wanted to be out of our comfort zone, and we are. Every challenge is a potential learning experience, a way to grow, or a faux pas so embarrassing that you want to disappear. Either way, you learn. No matter how well we speak, our accents give us away. We had hoped to pass for French, but that rarely happens. When we open our mouths to speak French, an American flag unfurls.

We notice that French women wear jeans and sneakers, which sometimes makes them difficult to distinguish from Americans. There was a time when no French woman—even one with bunions and hammertoes—would ever wear sneakers. She'd rather have her feet amputated.

Trying to make yourself at home in a place that is not home requires an aptitude for pretending. Happily, Larry and I share that talent. When I was a kid, after a Saturday matinee of *Breakfast at Tiffany's*, I'd be Audrey Hepburn, swanning about town until the spell broke. To this day, Larry will speak with a British accent after viewing an English film. The effect usually wears off within fifteen minutes, by which time we're literally back to ourselves.

It makes his day when Larry manages to fool an American woman in need of directions, who approaches him while he is painting a watercolor of Lou Clapas. Pronouncing each syllable slowly, loudly, and with care, she asks him, "Do you speak English?"

"I speek a leetle," Larry replies.

We try, Larry and I, to speak a leetle French to each other when we're at home or otherwise alone together. Clearly, that's the way to make the most of our French lessons. We start out with the best of intentions, but after a few minutes, we break down, at a literal loss for words. We've got certain phrases and thoughts down pat, like, "I'm hungry," or, "Did you finish your homework," but an intimate, adult relationship cannot thrive for long at a fifth-grade level.

However, when we're out on the street, and when we think we're walking near Americans, Larry and I will automatically switch from speaking English to pretending to speak fluent

French. Under the cover of anonymity, we let it rip, inventing French words, throwing proper verb endings to the winds, and tossing in an occasional *"Voilà!"* Americans are the only people we can hope to fool, assuming that they're even overhearing us, which they're probably not.

It is pitifully important to us that both they and we see us as French—*they* being other Americans, normal Americans who are not pretending to be French. At times like this, we don't think of ourselves as pretentious snobs, although perhaps we should. Instead, we feel more like children who know they're pretending when they say, "Let's play house." When we "play French," we also know we're pretending.

It Loses in Translation

Eating out is one of the great pleasures of Provençal life. Unlike tourists, we are in one locale long enough to find and revisit our favorite restaurants near our French home. Some we choose more for the conversation than the food, because we know that the proprietor will stop by our table to talk. Being recognized as regulars is a very good way to feel French. But sometimes we like to explore farther afield. Bob and Ellen have recommended the Bistro Lyonnais in Avignon. We look forward to another opportunity to speak French.

Larry calls to make a *réservation*. Linguistically this is not a difficult job. *"Je voudrais faire une réservation pour deux,"* he says. Larry frequently mispronounces "two" as *"Dieu,"* as in, "I would like to make a reservation for God." Luckily this time he gets it right.

The gentleman who takes our reservation answers back in English. "A table for two. What day and hour?"

"Samedi soir à vingt heures," Larry insists.

"Fine," the annoying Frenchman answers "We'll see you Saturday night at eight o'clock."

"A bientôt," says Larry, sticking to his guns.

"See you soon," says the Francophone killjoy.

Larry hates it when he is so easily unmasked. It doesn't occur to us that just as we want to practice our French, M. Yves Meduan, proprietor and *chef de cuisine*, may want to practice his English.

A similar war of words ensues on Saturday night when M. Meduan greets us at the door of his bistro.

"Welcome," he says, offering a hand to shake. "You must be the friends of the Greeneisens."

"Oui," says Larry. *"Ils nous ont recommandé votre restaurant."*

"Well," he says, "I hope you will be pleased with their recommendation."

And so it goes, this no-love-lost game of linguistic tennis: he lobs one over in very good English, and we lob one back in serviceable French. He shows us to our table.

We order in French while M. Meduan comments on our various choices in English.

"*Le poulet à la crème de champignons.*" When dining out, I frequently order chicken since Larry won't eat it at home.

"Very good," says M. Meduan. "I think you'll enjoy the mushroom cream sauce."

"*Pour commencer,*" says Larry, "*le foie gras.*"

"Our goose liver is the finest," says M. Meduan. "Enjoy it while you can. Soon you'll be back in America where it's getter harder and harder to find. There are *anti foie gras* societies like People for the Ethical Treatment of Animals in Provence," he tells us, "but they have little influence here." The French love their *foie gras,* a delicacy achieved by force-feeding a duck or goose until its liver is grossly enlarged, a process called *gavage.*

Force-feeding has a very bad press in America, but we wonder. Is *gavage* akin to a bulimic binge toward which a duck might waddle, as I would toward a Mars Bar, or is it more like water-boarding, away from which a duck might flap and flee? Ducks and geese, after all, are not people. Their esophagi are more flexible than those of humans. The results of studies, involving duck and goose control groups—but no fine-feathered focus groups—have been conclusive; nevertheless, the practice has been banned in many places.

While on a trip to the Dordogne in 1985, Larry and I witnessed a *gavage.* We were expecting to be horrified, but the moment the farmer appeared with his *gavage* pump, these birds of a feather flocked together around him, as eager as Pavlov's dog for the reward of having a tube inserted down their throats and their stomachs filled with maize. Was it masochism or genuine pleasure these geese were exhibiting at the prospect of being overfed? It is this experience that has convinced Larry to indulge his taste for the silky, fatty texture and mild liver taste of *foie gras.* He also indulges in cholesterol reducing drugs.

The bistro is small, and the tables are close together. M. Meduan, we soon learn, is no ordinary *propriétaire.* He is a devout believer in the inseparability of good food and good company. He moves boisterously from table to table, introducing the diners to one another, including us, *les Américains.* Soon we are talking from table to table. Again, as so often happens, we are complimented on our French. We are praised more for trying than for succeeding. They are delighted that we love Provence so much and that we have visited twice in the past two years, a month at a time.

Meanwhile, M. Meduan makes periodic visits from the kitchen to reassure himself that all his guests are getting along nicely and to tell an occasional joke. One, which I don't quite understand, is clearly an off-color joke followed by much laughter and more spontaneous joke telling. It becomes clear that someone at each table is offering a joke and that it will soon be our turn.

By now Larry and I have consumed an entire bottle of red and are speaking French fluently. Or maybe we're not. I am so full of *bonhomie* that I surprise myself by launching into a joke without having any idea of whether the pun, that is the punch line of the joke in English, is a *vrai* or *faux ami.* The joke involves a guy who sits down at bar and orders a drink. While he's sipping his *apéritif,* he keeps hearing little voices whispering sweet nothings in his ear. They love his necktie, the way he wears his hair, his suit. They tell him he's very good looking, très beau. But the man can't locate the source of these flattering words. There is no one else at the bar. Confused, he asks the bartender to identify the speakers. "Oh," says the bartender, "those are the complimentary peanuts." *"Ce sont les cacahuètes complimentaires."*

My punch line is met with total silence. Granted, it's not much of a joke in any language, but still. As I had feared, *"Ce sont les cacahuètes complimentaires"* doesn't *marche* in French. *Complimentaire* is a *faux ami.* It does not mean "flattering," as the joke requires. M. Meduan, once my bilingual pain in the neck, now my linguistic savior, immediately intervenes and explains to my fellow diners why my joke is both incomprehensible and unfunny. Nevertheless, the diners applaud me enthusiastically, surely more for my courage than for my wit, but I am too drunk to care. I have just told an entire joke, albeit a dud, with something resembling fluency. Besides, I remembered how to say "peanut."

We have a history of traveling disasters, many of them linked to restaurants. Eating out had a different meaning when we camped through Europe in the 1960s and cooked our meals outdoors, but every so often we'd treat ourselves to an indoor meal.

One night, while driving through the tiny French town of Talloires near the Swiss border, Larry spotted a small restaurant that looked like a chalet. A little on the corny side, we agreed, but what do you expect when you're that close to a country that hides money, yodels, and plays the spoons? We'd give it a try.

Just in case they had a dress code, we got our backpacks out of the trunk of the VW bug, where, for special occasions, Larry kept a pair of khakis, and I had a rolled up skirt. We found some roadside shrubs to hide behind and changed.

We took a seat at one of the small tables on the patio. Even though it was seven in the evening, nobody else was there. We sat down and waited. I was beginning to wonder if this was going to be like our misadventure in Athens where we tried to check into a hospital, thinking it was a hotel. Maybe this chalet was a private home? Most of the time when we were camping and we wanted to sleep cheap and indoors, we had no trouble spotting hotels. In France, we looked for the word *pension* over the door of a building; in Italy, *pensione*. When we crossed over the border into Greece, we forgot that Greek was Greek to us. No wonder the man we first thought was the concierge was dressed in whites and wore a stethoscope.

Eventually a waiter in formal attire arrived, greeted us, and waited at attention until we each ordered a glass of wine. When he returned with the wine and the bill, the total of which exceeded our entire dinner budget, we considered making a run for it.

Shortly thereafter, a handsome, middle-aged gentleman dressed in a dinner jacket walked toward us and introduced himself. After some cordial conversation in English, he told us that he and his wife had just flown in from South Africa for the sole purpose of dining at this restaurant. The gentleman asked us in the nicest possible way if we had any idea where we were. We didn't. He allowed as how he thought so.

We were at Père Bise, he explained, a three-star restaurant and inn, one of the finest in Europe. He bought us another round of drinks, tipped the waiter, and wished us a bon voyage. Later that night, we shared a ham sandwich in our sleeping bags.

WE DON'T LIKE TOURS; WE LISTEN IN ON YOURS

We lead double lives in Provence. One role is French—the part that lives in a house, attends classes, and gives parties. We even break the law. Ulli leads us to an abandoned ochre mine, where swimming is not permitted, but we swim nevertheless. The other role is tourist. On the days that we don't have class, we tend to go touring.

Larry and I have an ambivalent relationship to tourism, given that we don't want to be what we so obviously are—tourists. You can't go to Paris without visiting Notre Dame. It's required. Then, if you like, you may retire to a café and a glass of wine. And you can't go to Provence without visiting the Papal Palace in Avignon.

We are constantly weighing the advantages of succumbing to guided or even self-guided tours in a town or city we don't know, versus the instinct to wander aimlessly through a town or city in the hope that we will somehow take in its essence without a more focused, studied effort.

We are wary of tours, partly because we so often find them disappointing. We don't care how tall buildings are or how many tons of stone from wherever went into their construction. We cringe at the prospect of being herded from one place to another, although, to be fair, we are not above hovering at the fringes of the tour group trying to hear what the guide is saying, particularly if she's saying it in English.

For us, guidebooks are mainly for casing the joint. We follow them at least to the door of the recommended church or palace, but most often we don't enter. From years of travel, we've concluded that we can't trust the guidebooks' star-struck recommendations. We let our guard down and pay over 10 euros each to enter the three-star Papal Palace in Avignon. In contrast to its exterior towers, arches, and crenellations—which you can enjoy for nothing—the interior is bleak and bare—a giant snore.

We tend to avoid the monuments and delight in the small stuff—a massive lion's head doorknocker, intricate iron grillwork, a timeworn threshold. We prefer to walk around the medieval walls of Avignon, where retired men play boules, and old women sit on the benches and chat. People, not places, interest us most. We hang around the players, hoping they will invite us to join the game. That's what we want, brief encounters of the human kind.

Roussillon is one of the officially designated *plus beau villages* of Provence. The independent *Association des Plus Beaux*

Villages de France does not look into a mirror to determine which are the fairest of them all; they rely on objective criteria. The village population should be no more than two thousand, and the village should have at least two classified sites of scientific, artistic, or historic interest. There are about 150 such villages in all of France, seven of them in the Vaucluse. Six are hill towns— Ansouis, Gordes, Rousillon, Seguret, Venasque, and Mènerbes. The seventh is flat and lovely Lourmarin.

Rousillon is most famous for being perched on a precious lode of earth pigmented by shades of ochre that span the color palette from intense golden yellow to blood red.

We visit first by car; it's almost impossible to find a parking space. On another day, we tackle the climb by bike. We wander the streets, enjoying the colorful hues of stores and houses. We order a cup of coffee in the center of town, across from the church. We chat up the waiter. What we don't do is the obvious: we don't take the tour through the Sentiers des Ochres, the old ochre mines. The tour brochure tells us that the Romans started to export ochre powder from the area over two thousand years ago and that until 1930, when synthetic colors took over the world-wide market, one thousand people were employed in the ochre mines.

"The tour might be interesting," says Larry, trying out the idea.

"This whole town is ochre," I respond. "Who needs to see more ochre?" So much for Roussillon.

We also snub tourism in Gordes—not to be confused with Goult. Gordes is probably the most popular tourist town and the most precariously perched village in our part of Provence. It, too, is a designated a plus beaux village. It clings to a plateau overlooking the Luberon Valley. We try, but we cannot even visit Gordes as tourists, never mind wander without purpose through its narrow streets. We can only admire the stamina and intellectual curiosity of those visitors who persist. We hope that they found a parking place. We hope they could make their way past the anachronistic fleet of enamel-shiny tourist busses the size of railroad cars that park in the center of town on narrow streets intended for horse-drawn carts and obscure the view of the medieval houses, most of them now souvenir shops. We hope their visit to the fifteenth-century castle at the top of the town and the adjacent great hall with its "magnificently decorated Renaissance fireplace" was worth the climb. We tried to get there on our first and only visit to Gordes, but we gave up, overwhelmed by the mob of which we were a part.

Still, we *have* found a way to love Gordes—from afar. When we drive by, we sometimes pull over to the side of the road and get out of the car to admire the town. It is dramatically located at a curve in the road, girdled at its base by steep, supporting terraces, as if to keep it from collapsing. The houses seem to lean against one another for support. They are piled in ever-smaller tiers like a wedding cake of golden limestone blocks. A castle sits on the smallest tier, its narrow spire exclaiming the top of the town. Viewed from the roadside, hundreds of feet below, the town sheds its touristic trappings and retreats into its historical origins. We must tilt our heads back to take in the whole magnificent scene. For us, Gordes is a *plus beau*, three-star drive-by photo op.

By contrast, we find, much to our surprise, that we are happy to be tourists at the underrated Michelin one-star L'Abbaye de Notre Dame de Senanque. This twelfth-century structure is an architectural treasure set deep in an isolated rocky valley near Gordes. We approach her from on high, by way of a downward winding, narrow, one-lane road, so perilous that drivers heading down the canyon must pull into passing places in order not to collide with traffic climbing out of the canyon. Her singular location is part of her charm; she plays hard to get to, but she's easy on the eyes. Because we're here in July, our panoramic view includes acres of lavender fields in full, voluptuous bloom.

We walk around the chaste exterior, admiring her austere lines. Unlike so many architectural beauties, barred by fences or velvet ropes, the abbey is approachable. We can get close enough to touch her, to stroll alongside her, letting our fingers play along her smooth, heather-gray stone. These blocks bear the signatures—the individual marks, actually—of the masons who cut them. The workers were paid by the block. One such mark is a B lying on its side; another is a snaillike design. Who was this man, I wonder, who made his mark with a B? Did the other mason perhaps have a sense of humor and a taste for escargots? I trace each one with my finger.

We decide to take the guided tour in French. We could have opted for English, but then we wouldn't be French, would we?

We suffer the appropriate punishment for our presumption. We see much that is interesting, but we barely understand a word.

Properly humbled, the next time we visit the abbey, we take the tour in English. Particularly fascinating are the Brobdignagian building tools used in its construction. They hang, in all their gigantic, primitive utility, looking dark and dangerous against the pale, vaulted walls they helped to build: the double saws that cut the limestone; the monster tongs used to move them. This is one of the moments, as they say, that history comes alive. For an instant, I can see through time. My twelfth-century avatar is there, watching two men, one at each end of the saw, alternately pull and push against the limestone. I feel their enormous effort as stone turns to dust at their feet. Time travel is the ultimate in touring. The farther back we can go, the more profoundly we belong.

We are escorted to the Cistercian monks' dormitory where they used to sleep, fully dressed, separated from the cold stone floor by straw. We visit the Charter Room, the only place in the abbey where the monks are allowed to speak, and the scriptorium, the only heated room, a necessary concession to austerity; frozen fingers cannot write. In order not to tempt the eye, the arcades of the cloisters are decorated by a simple leaf pattern. How ironic that we find the purity and simplicity of this virginal place so ravishing.

We cannot get enough of her. We walk through the abbey, stopping at each exhibit to read the accompanying English translation. Actually, we try to read the French first and then supplement our understanding by reading the English. Our sojourns in Provence often feel as if we are watching an endless movie in French, with English subtitles.

The next time we visit the abbey, we are ready to make ourselves at home. We bring our French lessons and a picnic dinner. Monique has recommended that we attend vespers. They are open to the public, but hardly anyone knows it. We wait on the hillside, where we have a fine view of the abbey and of the crowds of people eager to find out if the inside of this lovely monument to pure thoughts is equally beautiful on the inside.

It is six in the evening, time for vespers, which take place in a vaulted, austere, beautifully proportioned Romanesque chapel. Light, the only luxury, pours into three deep-cut windows, illuminating the altar around which a few monks, dressed in white robes, are gathered. We are the only guests that day. We sit way in the back so that we can exit without calling attention to ourselves. We have never heard live Gregorian chants before. Sometimes the monks sing together; other times responsively. Sometimes they sit, sometimes they stand; often they bow. The chants rise and echo as they fill the vaulted dome. We are spiritually transported. But when it comes to the sermon, we're out of there, body and soul.

We visit Cavaillon, a city known for its delicious melons and for being the major produce market in our area. We pass Cavaillon often on our way to Avignon before we actually visit the place. It is impossible to drive by without noticing the sculpture of a melon the size of a house, which rests on its side on a pedestal on its own esplanade, marking the route into Cavaillon.

Each time, we inevitably collaborate on making up a story about the fictional artist who made the melon. We give him a name, Pierre Le Melon. We give him a life. He is a poor but talented sculptor, someone who sees himself as a serious artist, maybe not quite in the ranks of Rodin but certainly a lot more worthy than a mere sculptor of melons.

He almost doesn't accept the commission from the dimwitted town fathers who insist upon a melon, but frankly, Pierre and his wife, Marianne, can't afford not to accept the commission. Nor can Pierre bear to admit to his wife, who believes in his greatness, that he spends his days carving a nine-ton melon, with stem. Oh the shame of it! He doesn't tell her, leaving her free to think he's out sculpting something as lofty as the *Pietà*, or at the very least, the *David*. But ultimately, Pierre cannot avoid his wife's inevitable question.

"What did you sculpt today, my dear Pierre?"

"Please," replies Pierre, covering his shame in rueful mystery, "don't ask."

Sometimes we change the story so that Pierre loves sculpting the melon, and his wife thinks it's a work of genius. In another version of our story, the melon breaks loose from its pedestal and goes rolling through the town of Cavaillon, squashing everything in its path, including melons.

Eventually we break down and take the recommended self-guided walking tour through the older part of the city, Vieux Cavaillon, which includes a number of wonderfully ruined stone façades, among them a first-century arch, and an eighteenth-century synagogue.

We get more Jewish whenever we're somewhere besides home. In the fourteenth century, when Pope Clément V established himself in Avignon, the Jewish residents of four towns in the Vaucluse enjoyed his "protection": Carpentras, Avignon, L'Isle sur la Sorgue, and Cavaillon. These people were known as "Les Juifs du Pape," "the Pope's Jews." At first having the pope's blessing was a good deal; Jews were free to live, worship, and work as they wished. Then ethnic tensions mounted. Jews were banished from the professions and confined to ghettoes. Men were forced to wear a yellow hat; women a yellow bit of cloth. Yellow. A very bad omen.

There is a street in L'Isle sur la Sorgue called, matter-of-factly, Place de la Juiverie, the Jewish Quarter, a reminder of the ghetto and of a less tolerant time. Happily, we haven't detected any anti-Semitism among the people we've met, but anti-Muslim sentiments are offered up freely to total strangers. In Cavaillon, we enter a shop. I have seen a sweater in the window that I can't be French without. The usual conversation ensues. "Where are you from?" We tell. "You speak very well." We thank. But the conversation changes radically when the shopkeeper notices two Muslim women in burkas passing by.

"They are the ruin of France," she says. "They've got to go."

It used to be the Jews; now they minor in Jews and major in Muslims. It's always somebody.

Near the end of the tour of Cavaillon, we are drawn by ethereal choral music to a small, twelfth-century cloister where a variety of flowers form a rectangle in the center, blooming bright against the luminous beige limestone of the arched passageways. We follow the music that emanates from the adjacent cathedral, where we pause to wait with an elegantly dressed crowd that has gathered in a state of happy expectation outside the cathedral door, waiting for something to happen. The doors swing open, and a bride and groom emerge, arm in arm, in all their veiled and tuxedoed glory, smiling and waving at their guests. The guests smile and applaud. We smile and applaud vigorously. We are no longer tourists. We're members of the wedding.

Next door to the church, we come upon a preschool playground. It must be recess. In one corner, a little Vidal Sassoon wannabe, equipped with a comb, is styling a little girl's hair while she patiently awaits the results of his makeover. Near the swing sets, a gang of little boys and girls are chasing each other. Sometimes a boy will chase another boy and wrestle him to the ground. Sometimes a little boy will chase a little girl, wrestle her to the ground, lay on top of her, and kiss her on the lips. The little girls appear to be kissing back, ardently. Are the French born that way? Is it nature or nurture?

We never fail to crack a joke when we drive or cycle past a road sign pointing in the direction of St. Pantaléon. "St. Pants," we call it. St. Pants doesn't even get a mention in our guidebook, a dumb fact that attracts our perverse attention. A village with nothing to recommend it? So much the better. We huff and puff our way through the countryside, heading toward our no-count village.

After a couple of uphill kilometers, we come upon a sign indicating that a glass museum can be found further down a dirt pathway. Without needing to consult each other, we turn onto the pathway, get off our bikes, and start walking. Within seconds, we find ourselves surrounded by a weird forest of abstract shapes, some taller than we, made of colored shards of glass and twisted metal.

We stop at various points along the pathway to examine one or another of these tormented forms. I do what I always do when surrounded by art I do not appreciate. I try to like it. I blame myself for being such a dolt. I'm in a museum after all. I conclude that there must be something wrong with me. Then, after feeling inadequate for as long as I can stand to— maybe a couple of seconds—I change my mind and speak with the authority of Phillipe de Montebello. "This is not art," I pronounce. "Some psychopath off his meds must have found himself with lots of time and an excess of broken glass, axels, and hubcaps." But what do I know? Don't be surprised if some day you find his work on display in the Modern Museum of Art.

At the end of this bizarre pathway, we see what must be the museum dug into the hillside. It looks more like an underground bunker. We sense the possibility of adventure, and it appears, personified, at the doorway. She is the guardian of the place.

By the overjoyed welcome she gives us, we suspect she's been waiting hours for anybody to show up.

She escorts us into the lobby. She doesn't even try to sell us a ticket to the exhibit. She is desperate to talk. So are we.

Larry and I differ in our opinions of how well we speak. I don't think our French is all that good. Larry does. Larry is a far more optimistic person than I am. He'd rather be happy. I'd rather be right.

Still, we get along. Béatrice—we're on a first-name basis—used to have an American boyfriend, but she's forgotten most of her English. She fills in with French words when we falter. We fill in with English when she's at a loss. Our mutual desire to talk bonds us almost instantly and keeps us conversing until closing time, prior to which nobody visits the museum. We exchange e-mail addresses and cheerful *à bientôts*, but we know, and she knows, we'll never be in touch again. We score another delightful hit-and-run friendship. We are at our faux finest.

WE'RE PARTY ANIMALS

The Provençaux love festivals. They celebrate lavender, grapes, guitars, boats, music, rivers, gardens, wine, the roots of the vines, folklore, cheese, dogs, rocks, and much, much more—and that's not even counting local saints. At our real home, there's an oyster festival every June and an Italian festival in the fall, but do we ever go? No. But here, because we are determined to live *la vie Provençale*, we do. Be it ever so humble, there's no place like somewhere else.

Monique encourages Larry and me, along with Ulli and Bettina and our goddaughter, Zoe, who's visiting from California, to attend La Féerie Nautique in L'Isle. The Féerie is really just a warm-up, a prelaunching launching celebration to congratulate all the workers who have designed and built fanciful floats that will parade down the Sorgue River the following month. The one that gets the most attention is a very large replica of the *Mayflower*. The young man who made it proudly explains to us that he has used wire fencing for an armature and then layered on lots of plaster and papier-mâché. He plans to string it with lights for the big event. His boat will be a splendid sight on the river.

At least 150 townspeople are admiring the floats and enjoying the punch. Children are passing around plates of pale pizzalike triangles of *pissaladière*, loaded with onions, chunks of *saucisson de sanglier*, wild boar sausage, and *anchois*. Monique and Ange introduce us all to as many villagers as they know. We are welcomed as if we were foreign dignitaries. Yet again, we are astounded and warmed by the enthusiasm with which we strangers are greeted. In the following week's issue of the regional newspaper, *La Provence*, our presence at the La Féerie is noted (with special mention going to *"Zoe, la jolie californienne."*)

A woman, one of the organizers of La Féerie, reads a message of welcome and praise from the mayor. The message consists primarily of a Homeric naming of all of the people in the trades—the electricians, masons, builders, cabinet makers, and many more—who have contributed their time and labor to building the floats. When we attend events at home, it is the sponsors of events who are honored in the program, listed in declining financial categories—platinum, gold, and silver. This festival in L'Isle sur la Sorgue seems closer to the heart. Here we sense a communal thrill. Perhaps the difference we note is the distinction between the intimacy of village life and the relative isolation of suburban living. Festivals in Vermont villages, I suspect, may be more like this one.

At the end of the ceremony, everyone—workers and townspeople—line up, some standing, some sitting on bleachers, for a group picture, a scene that reminds me of an end-of-camp or elementary school photo session. The townspeople insist that we be included. "Non, non," we protest. There is no way that we belong in this picture. We are outsiders, foreigners. But they prevail. *"Dites ouistiti,"* says the photographer. *"Ouistiti,"* Ange explains, is the French version of "Say cheese." It means marmoset. It's the *"stiti"* part of the word that stretches the corners of the mouth up into a smile. "Wee-stee-tee," we say in unison.

From a celebration of wet water, we party on to a celebration of dry rocks, held in our hometown, Saumane, where Le Festival des Pierres Seches, dry rocks, is an annual three-day event. It's held on the expansive backyard of the de Sade castle. We tramp up the hill. A rock festival? Why not? Limestone is the DNA of Provence.

We join many others as we file past an outdoor museum—hung with drawings and photographs featuring stone walls and *bories*, the primitive, beehive-shaped stone dwellings characteristic of Provence. About three thousand, dating from at least the Bronze Age, are scattered over the landscape. Some are large and rectangular and housed families as late as the nineteenth century. The smallest of the igloo-shaped bories sheltered shepherds or were used for storage. We've been fascinated by bories since we caught our first glimpse. I am drawn to the primitive. I want to know how it all started. I want to know what early people called home. I'm a sucker for caves, yurts, igloos, and teepees; to them I add bories.

Whether it's out of a passion for their history or a desire to attract tourists, or both, the French have enacted laws that new houses, many of which are built of modern cinderblock, must be faced in stone. Even the windows must replicate the dimensions of former times. As a result, stone is at a premium. Danielle, our Saumane neighbor, serves on a committee that is dedicated to protecting the ancient stone walls. People steal the stones for their private use.

Stonewalls in the Vaucluse are even more evident than the seventeenth-century dry stone walls in our native New England. Our earliest farmers cleared stones from the land in order to plow and plant. The resulting dry stone walls served as property lines. Some of them still exist near where we live, meandering in a semicollapsed state through the third growth woods and few open fields on which houses have not yet been built.

Walls in the Vaucluse, we learn, served multiple purposes. The ones with little recessed sections doubled as installations for beehives; those with vertical rocks on top discouraged animals from climbing over them; stone walls with vertical rocks set on the bottom allowed for drainage. We were particularly captivated by the grim evidence of Le Mur de la Peste, the plague wall, built around 1721 in the vain hope that it would quarantine the region from the bubonic plague.

At Le Festival des Pierres Sèches, it is stones all day and a rock concert in the evening, featuring Beatles music. The musicians are hippie French guys who look like refugees from the Haight—blue-jeaned, barefooted, and ponytailed.

At first, we, along with the rest of the crowd, sit on fold-out chairs placed in a semicircle several yards from the temporary stage, but within minutes, many of us are up on our feet, dancing and singing. We start out dancing with one another, but pretty soon we're cavorting with strangers—men, women, children— anyone who'll have us.

The French band is singing songs from the *White Album* in perfect English. It's impossible to tell if they've memorized the lyrics or if they actually know what they're saying. The audience sings along in English, too.

What French lyrics do I know? "Frère Jacques," for one, although up until much too recently, I used to fake-sing the third line, "Sonny Lemontina," which sounds more like a mafia don than a lyric from a French children's ditty. But now, after a couple of months of French language study, I know better. It's

"*Sonnez les Matines,*" ring the morning bells. I also know the first two lines of "La Marseillaise" and two lines of "Sur le pont d'Avignon." Whenever we drive along the banks of the Rhône in Avignon, we serenade what's left of it.

When the Faux Beatles start to play "Ob-La Di, Ob la Da," I find myself dancing and singing the chorus with great gusto. What sounds like English to my dancing partner, who's singing the same lyric, sounds like French to me.

We wouldn't miss the nighttime Marche Flottante de L'Isle sur la Sorgue, the annual watery pageant of nego-chin down the Sorgue River. The parade starts on the outskirts of town and ends in the bassin. About forty of Alain's hand-made boats, manned by Alain and his merry club of fisherman, dressed in traditional wide-brimmed black hats, white blouses, black vests and trousers, pole down the Sorgue. Adding to their number are several women, among them Alain's elder daughter, costumed in Provençal skirts and blouses. The flotilla comes to a stop in front of Café Bellevue, their blazing torches reflected in the quivering skin of the night-black water. All is still. Then, at a signal, the fishermen cast their nets wide into the bassin and sing the nineteenth-century Occitan Provençal national anthem written by Frédéric Mistral, a cappella. Their voices are strong and proud.

I have no idea what they are singing, but no matter. I am transported. Standing at the bassin, my hand on my fast-beating heart, my eyes fill with tears. I am a slut for patriotism. Anybody's patriotism.

WHAT'S SHE GOT THAT I HAVEN'T?

When I'm out and about in the towns of the Vaucluse, I study the attractive women walking toward me. Usually they stare back brazenly. Neither of us blinks. We lock eyes until we must either stop and meet, face-to-face, or pass out of one another's view forever. In those few seconds of contact, I conduct a body search. I probe for her secrets. I quickly slip in and out of her skin. When a man does what I'm doing, it's called being on the make. When I womanize, I am trying to identify that certain *je ne sais quoi* that French women are supposed to have. Without that knowledge, how can I possibly pretend to be French?

I am a true believer in the lie that change can come from the outside in, so I've set out to buy a dress. Monique has given me the name of her favorite store in Avignon. It's late June, and the fields of *les tournesols*, sunflowers that literally turn to the sun, make the familiar forty-minute drive a treat. Van Gogh's vision of Provence is so imprinted on my brain that it is as if the place didn't exist before he painted it. I cannot help but see the irises, the cedars, the sunflowers, the blazing blue sky, and the limestone cliffs through the lens of his manic vision. Provence is resplendent with memories of color.

I work my way through rack after rack of dresses, examining each one briefly and dismissing it. I don't want anything too fancy. I wear jeans most of the time, so I'm looking for something practical. How often do I need a really fancy dress? Maybe once a year, and then I can always wear my black velvet pants and a silk shirt. Some part of me that does not wish me well is hell-bent on making what could be a genuine shopping spree into a joyless exercise in self-denial.

Another woman begins to look through the dresses alongside me. The slide of hangers on the metal rack, like beads on an abacus, and an occasional exchange of *excusez-moi* are the only sounds that accompany this universal female ritual called shopping.

I size her up through narrowing, gimlet eyes. What's she got that I haven't got? She's a size ten on top and at least a twelve on the bottom. She has one of those high, bony chicken chests to which breasts must take second place. I'm a well-proportioned eight all over, and I still have the vestiges of a waist. Her waist is thick, and her upper arms sway like swags. Mine are a bit droopy—I'm thinking about sticking to long sleeves—but they don't actually swing. Etched on both our faces are enough laugh lines to suggest that we've both been amused for at least six decades. Her hair is dirty blonde. It falls lank to her shoulders, emphasizing, it seems to me, her jowls. I have recently had my hair cut short for just that reason. I brush it upward, away from my face, to give me what my hairdresser calls "a lift." In the face department, we're a draw. When it comes to bodies, it's no contest.

I find a dress I like that I can afford. It's blue cotton with a pretty floral pattern and has a flattering boat neck, three-quarter-length sleeves, and a full skirt. It's belted at the waist—that could be a problem—but still, it's worth a try, and the price is right. My French counterpart ducks behind me and snaps up a dress I have pushed aside. It's a sleeveless red taffeta cocktail dress, with a neckline that plunges nearly all the way to the waistline, the same dress that I have just rejected as gorgeous but too revealing, too red, too expensive, too young for me, and besides, I don't need or deserve it. None of this appears to bother Ms. France.

I follow her into the dressing room. She struggles into the dress. Her *poitrine* rises like a Frank Perdue carcass from the red décolletage. She steps into her high heels.

She pirouettes in front of the mirror. The peplum bobbles comically on her wide hips. She places one foot forward at an angle to the other, slides her hands lovingly up and down her own flanks, rakes her fingers through her hair, tosses back her head, wets her lips, and puts the make on her own reflection in the mirror. What's she got that I haven't got? I think I know. It is the certain knowledge that she is beautiful. So what if she's wrong. She's happy, isn't she?

Besides, the longer she preens there, exuding a musk of *amour propre* more French than Chanel No. 5, the more beautiful she becomes. I, who just moments ago saw every line and bulge, now find myself viewing her through a more generous lens, as if she were backlit and I were filming her through chiffon. I find her conviction that she is beautiful utterly convincing. I am seduced, and I'm not even a consumer. I don't bother to try on the dress I've chosen. I don't like it anymore. It's too American.

Discouraged, I head back home. As I drive, I find myself thinking about a push-up bra and panties set, both fashioned to look like an artichoke, that I paused to make fun of when I saw them in the window of a lingerie shop in the center of L'Isle. Each green nylon leaf overlapped the next as they circled ever closer to the nipple. The thong panties were a mere triangle of leaves.

How comical! How verging on obscene! *Even Victoria's Secret wouldn't go so far as to try to make an artichoke sexy*, I thought at the time. But now, after my failure to buy the red dress, I'm not so sure. Maybe if I want to look like a French woman, I've got to feel like a French woman, right down to my underwear. Maybe I've got to go vegetal.

I park the car near Catherine's real estate office, where there's almost always a space, pop my head in to say *"Bonjour,"* and walk along the canal to the center of town.

"Les sous-vêtements d'artichaut?" the saleswoman says without cracking a smile. *"Ils sont très populaires."* If artichoke underwear is *très populaires* with French women, I am determined that it is going to be *très populaire* with me.

Once home, I put on the bra and panties only to find that the dark green leaves show through my clothes—as does the concentric structure, which looks bunchy under a T-shirt. Apparently, when you wear artichoke underwear you're not supposed to be wearing clothes.

I try the outfit on for Larry. I strike a fetching, slightly slouchy pose, hands on hips, my right foot a bit forward like the models do.

"I'd rather eat them dipped in lemon butter" is his response.

I have blown almost thirty euros on something I'll never wear. I have also learned an important lesson about that certain *je ne sais quoi*. I don't have it.

⚷

PROUST BRINGS COOKIES TO DINNER

Because we are nearing the end of our second stay in Saumane, all Mo's students, plus Monique and Ange, decide to splurge and go out together for a farewell dinner. We choose Le Mas de Tourteron in the nearby town of Imberts. The night air is soft and balmy. The place surprises us with its beauty. The old, blue-shuttered stone farmhouse where the food is prepared serves as a seventeenth-century backdrop to the white-clothed tables set in a fairyland garden of lawn, flowers, and twinkling white lights. From where we are seated, Larry has a perfect view into one of the rectangular kitchen windows in which he swears he sees, as if framed, a living replica of the famous portrait of a Vermeer kitchen maid wearing a white linen cap on her head, pouring milk from a pitcher. The evening feels full of promise.

We haven't given much thought to the linguistic composition of the group, but when we are all seated around the table, we realize that we have inadvertently assembled our own little UN

Security Council, only without the headphones. A newcomer to our class, Margarit, who is German, wants to brush up her almost perfect French. She also speaks some English. Margarit has brought her husband, Willhelm, who speaks nothing but German. That's fine for Ulli and Bettina, and even Mo, who speaks some German, but it renders Larry, me, and Ange speechless, at least if we want to talk with Willhelm.

Willhelm tries valiantly to engage with those of us who speak no German, which he has to do via Margarit, who then translates his words into either French or English, so that Larry, Ange, and I can understand.

The food is delicious, especially the lamb, redolent of the thyme that grows abundantly where the lambs pasture. Even innocent lambs make a contribution to French gastronomy by seasoning themselves. But a beautiful setting and a delicious meal do not make up for the fact that we are in danger of splintering into exclusive, linguistic comfort zones, a serious affront to one of the most important of French cultural standards, the interdependence of food and sociability.

Monique comes to the rescue. She would like to propose a game. *"Ein spiel,"* she tells Willhelm. Monique, in her clearest French, made even more comprehensible by a choreography of hand charades that almost speak for themselves, evokes the memory of Proust and his most famous book, *A La Recherche du Temps Perdu*, a title I immediately associate with laundry.

Monique asks us, again in French, with gestures, if we've all read it. Everybody nods or shakes his or her head, including me.

I have not. I tried, but I gave up. Nevertheless, the book speaks volumes as a cultural reference to everyone at the table. We've all heard of that little cookie, *la madeleine*, which triggers for the adult Proust a childhood memory of dipping one into a cup of tea. "No sooner had the warm liquid mixed with the crumbs touched my palate," he wrote, "than a shudder ran through me and I stopped, intent upon the extraordinary thing that was happening to me, an exquisite pleasure had invaded my senses ..." Monique, who undoubtedly *has* read Proust, calls these magical moments of involuntary memory *les madeleines*.

Mo asks each of us to think of a madeleine from our own lives, an instance when, for whatever reason, we are returned by a sight, a sound, a taste, a touch, or a smell to a time in our childhoods. Monique breaks the ice by telling us that lounging on soft cushions evokes the pleasant sensation of her plump grandmother who held and comforted her against her soft, ample bosom. Her mother, she explains, was skinny and bony.

Margarit confesses she is moved against her will when she hears one of the embarrassingly sentimental songs that her mother used to sing. Ulli, too, is suffused with feeling by the thrill of a particular song. One spoonful of farina sends Ange to his native Corsica. The smell of frying oil wafts Larry back to his parents' food stand on the boardwalk in Wildwood, New Jersey.

I recall being surprised one day while taking a walk to feel my eyes filling with tears, unbidden by any accompanying thought. Then I looked around and saw I was standing near a chain-link fence that was covered with honeysuckle. Its scent brought to mind my shy grandfather who used to take me for drives in his car, during which he hardly spoke to me. Still, there was always a sprig of honeysuckle in a tiny glass vase that hung from his rearview mirror, filling the car with sweetness.

The sight of a particular kind of trivet reunites Bettina with her grandmother and a special casserole she used to place upon it. Bettina tells us that her grandmother was confined to a wheelchair. I wonder if that's why Bettina works at a school for the handicapped.

Middle-aged Wilhelm fills with joy when he sees a flight of swallows. As a young boy, he would flush them skyward each time he rode past them on his bike to visit his beloved grandfather. He links his thumbs to mimic the flight of birds. He pedals his feet and pretends to shift gears to indicate a bike.

This polyglot evening, which lasts from eight until midnight, is a great success. We laugh with comprehension and delight in achieving such piercing intimacy. I don't know about the others, but Larry and I agree that we have been given a precious glimpse into the souls of each of these people, at least two of whom we hardly know.

If I ever see Willhelm again, I will think of swallows.

Broken and Entered

The day before we are to leave, someone breaks into our locked rental car, shatters the glass on the passenger side, and steals my purse. The car is parked in front of *les toilettes publiques*, a grungy port of last resort located in the center of L'Isle. I have left my purse in the car, because the floor of the public toilettes is not even someplace where you want to put your feet.

"I'll just be a sec," I tell Larry, "but if you leave the car, remember to lock it."

And that's what he does when he is seized by the urge to leave the car to study a menu posted in front of a restaurant across the street.

When I exit the toilet and see that Larry's not in the car, I'm ready to be angry, but I walk over to the passenger side and note that my pocketbook is on the floor and that the door is locked. I look around, spot Larry, and cross the street to join him.

We can't have spent more than a minute or two reading the menu and returning to the car, but it is long enough for a thief to hit and run, probably on a motor scooter. We didn't hear a thing.

We divide the nasty chores that lie ahead. I will cancel the credit card. Larry will report the theft at the police station. We'll meet back at Mo's house.

But first I must make an inventory to give to Larry to take to the *gendarmerie*, an in memoriam of the contents of my purse: My green wallet, so old that the leather has darkened and softened from my touch. I meant to keep it forever. Less sentimental but far more sickening is the loss of fifty euros and my Visa card. The thief is probably charging on it right now. Missing, too, is my driver's license—a pain in the ass to replace—all my class notes, a small plastic hairbrush—no big loss—and my supple, well-thumbed, well-loved, little yellow dictionary. Then, I almost forget, there's my cosmetic bag, which contains a tube of lipstick—actually, it will be fun to replace that with a French one—an emery board—shaggy nails drive me crazy—and a toothbrush and toothpaste—so do shaggy teeth. Oh, and a pill bottle full of Synthroid, an endocrine-balancing medication I take for hypothyroidism. Luckily, I've got some extras. The proper dose is one pill a day. Two will give you the jitters. I find myself hoping that the thief, thinking the stuff will make him high, swallows a fistful and suffers the effects of a serious overdose: tachycardia, confusion, seizures, strokes, coma, and death. Good. Let him have them all, and in that order. I am really pissed.

It's my job to cancel the credit card. I practice the relevant vocabulary: *annuler* means "cancel," and credit card is one of those loveable *vrais amis, carte de crédit*. I punch in a bunch of numbers that get me to an international French-speaking robot who offers me an incomprehensible list of options.

I press buttons. I yell "Visa" into the phone. Visa. It's got to be the same in French, right? Standing in the front of this wretched public bathroom, surrounded by broken glass, on the avenue Charles de Freaking Gaulle, I hate myself, I hate Larry, and I hate France. And then my cell phone runs out of juice.

In a panic of despair, I run off in *toutes directions* in search of Mo's house. *Grâce à Dieu*, she is home. While Ange effortlessly cancels my card, Monique brings me a glass of wine and listens to my French tale of woe. Now that I am no longer panicked,

I am remarkably fluent, and she is wonderfully empathetic, making periodic sounds of sympathy, *"La pauvre,"* "You poor thing," and, *"C'est la merde,"* "How shitty."

Meanwhile, Larry is at the *gendarmerie* where he is met by Officer Eric Federico with what Larry later describes as hostility concealed in the guise of official rectitude. He is sure Gendarme Federico is thinking, *Here comes another ugly, angry American. Did he buy a fake antique? Good. Serves him right.* And perhaps that is what Federico was thinking, but when Larry starts tossing around French words like *voleur,* thief, and sentences like *"La voiture était garée en face des toilettes publiques,"* "The car was parked in front of the public toilets," the gendarme is no longer hostile. He is kind, he is reassuring, he is even *désolé.* He explains to Larry that thieves usually remove only the money from purses and then throw the pocketbook, along with the rest of its contents, into a garbage bin. Does Larry have a local address to which he might return the pocketbook should it turn up? Larry gives him Mo's address, and, sure enough, a package containing my pocketbook with everything but the money will arrive three weeks after we are back home.

We are sad when this, our second month is over, so sad that we decide on the spot to return the following year. It is especially painful to say goodbye to Monique and to Ulli and Bettina. Ulli will continue to study French with Monique. She already speaks and writes French as well as we do.

"When we come back next year," I say to her on the last day of class, "you will be speaking French fluently, and we will still be speaking like children. Will we still be friends?" We both have tears in our eyes as we hug each other goodbye.

"Toujours," she says. "Always."

In the Third Place

Not So Nice

We have opted for a third season in the Vaucluse. We've decided to add some novelty to our adventure by flying from JFK to Nice instead of to Paris. We've never been to Nice, and we're particularly eager to explore the older section, Vieux Nice.

This search for novelty begins badly. First we have to drag our bags to the car rental. Then we have to wait an hour outside the rental office in the hammering Provençal sun to get the car we didn't specify. Then we get caught up in a maze of one-way streets that guarantee that you can't get there from here. We strain to read street signs. We ask directions. Our French is suffering from neglect. We drive in circles. We snap at each other. We can't find our hotel. When we do find it, we don't like it, and we especially don't like the fact that they don't offer parking, so we must reenter the maze and try to find a public parking garage. Then we can't find a decent place to eat dinner, then the bathroom is too small to share, and then we hate each other and go to bed.

After a good night's sleep, we're a team again, on a mission: find old Nice. It's got to be there somewhere. It's in Nice after all. But no matter how far we walk, no matter how many people we derange by asking for directions, we can't find it. When we finally do, our spirits are temporarily lifted by its narrow, winding streets, mottled stone walls, and pastel shutters.

Not surprisingly, there's a *fête* in Old Nice. This one is mostly about food, so Larry immediately buys some figs, cheese bread, and several triangles of *pissaladière*, loaded with onions and so much oil that it runs down our arms and drips off our elbows. I'm more interested in the impressive brace of oxen attached to a cart of hay and a demonstration of what I think is an oil press.

We hit the highway in the early afternoon, bound eastward toward the town of Goult, a town we had identified the year before as ideal for our third sojourn. The curvy, nineteenth-century art nouveau lettering on the awning of Le Café de la Poste in the center of town helped to seal the deal for me. Old signage fills me with pleasure. Best of all, this is a town that fewer tourists have discovered, probably because it's not directly visible from the highway. And since we're not tourists, we expect to feel right at home.

Unlike Saumane, Goult is a real town, bustling with commerce and loaded with mossy rocks, buried telephone wires, and other evidences of well-maintained antiquity. Narrow streets wind upward to a plateau where a windmill literally tops off this medieval *village perché*.

We would be twelve miles farther away from L'Isle, the Prétots, the Greeneisens, and Mo. However, we would be that much closer to Ulli and Bettina. Because of the extra distance from Mo, we decide to take two rather than three lessons a week. We tell ourselves it is the practical thing to do. Lessons are expensive. What we don't tell ourselves is that while we have not lost our enthusiasm for Mo or her engaging teaching style, we are losing our enthusiasm for anything that smacks of work, like studying.

When we leave Nice that afternoon, en route to Goult, the sun is so hot that the asphalt roads are licorice-sticky. As soon as we find our way out of the city and onto the highway, we are caught in what turns out to be a forty-five-minute traffic jam. "Beaucoup de circulation," says Larry. Lots of traffic. Later we learn that there's always a molar-grinding amount of noncirculating *circulation* on Saturdays on this particular highway, which leads to the popular destination of Aix as well as to Goult. We have forgotten the word for traffic jam, but I dig in my purse for my little yellow book and remind us both that, of course, it's *un bouchon*, directly related to Ange's *tire-bouchons*, his corkscrews. We are corked. Not a car has budged for ten minutes.

Lots of drivers get out of their cars, some to allow their dogs to pee. The French take their dogs everywhere, even to restaurants. Eventually, I get out, too, and stand on my tiptoes, along with many others, our hands shielding our eyes from the sun, trying to see if the cars in the far distance are moving. It's hard to tell, because the asphalt is sending up a mirage of heat waves that might be misconstrued as motion.

"*Ça bouge!*" the woman next to me says. She thinks the line is moving. I have been scanning the road ahead, too, and I am quite certain that the line is not *bouging*. I take a swan dive into the word pool of cognates and come up with, "*Non. Ça ne bouge pas; c'est une illusion opticale.*" As always, I am on the lookout for *vrais amis*. "*Il faut oser,*" is my motto. One must dare.

"*Non,*" she chooses to disagree. "*Ce n'est pas une illusion opticale.*"

She understands me. She might even take me for French. I am ridiculously proud of myself. Some people get a thrill from getting away with murder. I get mine from committing petty lingual larceny.

THE HOUSE SPEAKS ENGLISH

This is the first time we have rented a French house from an American couple. We have taken the virtual tour, so we're pretty sure we can't be disappointed. In addition to our well-worn map of the Vaucluse and our yellow dictionary, we carry with us a file full of driving directions, recommendations, and house instructions from the owners. The directions for the Saumane house were in French. These are in English, which, we are sorry to admit, makes them much easier to understand. Apparently English is still our first language.

We find the house without difficulty. As advertised, it is right on the square. The shutters are wine colored. The heavy wooden front door is flanked by stone pots filled with herbs. And even though I'm allergic to cats, I enjoy the sight of a French puss lounging on our next-door neighbor's windowsill. We spot a large snail making its slimy way along one of the rough stone steps leading to the door. I point it out to Larry. He bends to pick it up.

"Don't!" I cry. "Snails are good luck."

"Snails are escargots," he says. "A little garlic, a little butter, a splash of white wine, garnish with parsley—and *voilà!*" Larry's preoccupation with food can get a little out of control, but I'm grateful to be married to a man who loves to shop, cook, and empty the dishwasher.

One part of the house dates to the seventeenth century; the other was added in the nineteenth. We are charmed by the ravaged plaster facing of the oldest part of the house, scabs of which have peeled off in some places, revealing the ancient stone construction beneath. The further back we travel in time, the more French we feel. Coming from a country where Alcatraz is a national historic landmark and our most popular ruin, we long for the legitimacy of antiquity. This house delivers.

We ring the doorbell to summon the housekeeper. She is not quite finished readying the house and suggests that we put our bags inside, have a drink at Le Café de la Poste immediately across the square, and come back in about forty-five minutes.

We retire to the café where we encounter more disappointment. The original art nouveau signage on Le Café de la Poste's awning has been replaced by an alien, modern font. How dare they change the lettering on my sign!

From the café, we see the housekeeper gesturing to us. The house is ready. She hands us a large antique key. She demonstrates how it requires a bit of wiggling in the lock. She apologizes for the inconvenience. We don't mind. When we're in France, inconvenience is mother's milk to us.

We meet our house in Goult as if she were a mail-order bride. We understand how critical any house is to the success of being able to make ourselves at home. We must get along. We hope that she will work out, that she's as good as her picture.

The hallway may have been inauspicious at first glance, but the floors are terra-cotta, just the way we like them. The small hallway gives way to an Escher of a staircase that zigs and zags its way upward. We find ourselves staring in deep perplexity at the flat side of the back of the staircase to which is affixed a very large poster of a head of a man with an accordion for a mouth. We once rented a house for a week in San Gimignano. There was a picture in the dining room of a man holding his own intestines. We can definitely live with accordion man.

This place is stair city. There are forty-two of them in all. Three steps lead to the front door; three more steps to a small WC; four steps down to the salon. And that's just downstairs. To go upstairs, you Stairmaster your way up eleven more, counting the landing, and then, after a pivot to the left, another eleven stairs take you to the bedroom level, where you may lie down for a rest. This place is a workout, and I love it.

We introduce ourselves to each room. We follow the hallway a few steps down to the salon. On the wall hangs a TV screen much larger and more modern than ours at home. English-language DVDs and CDs are stacked on shelves below. The movies are in English; how tempting.

Larry chooses his favorite reading chair. I notice that the coffee table is the right size for Scrabble. On the back wall of the salon hangs a reproduction of the iconic self-portrait of local hero Vincent Van Gogh. Where Van Gogh's head should be rests the head of a cat, with two fully intact ears. I'm beginning to appreciate their quirky sense of humor. Besides, we are occupying someone else's life. Isn't that the point?

The kitchen is a lot larger than our kitchen in Saumane but still smaller than our kitchen at home. Small kitchens are one of the marvels of French cuisine. Apparently, like sex, the other reputed French preoccupation, size doesn't matter. And it's very well equipped. At last here's the Cuisinart Larry's been missing! Clearly the American owners of this house like to cook. Larry is delighted.

No matter which house we're renting, it is important that I identify what will be my favorite coffee cup. I have a favorite cup at home, too. I will read the kitchen shelves, carefully examining all the variations on the theme of cup—large mugs, small mugs,

mugs with trigger handles, teacups. I will pick them up, test their weight, capacity, color, size, and degree of comfort in my hand. As much as I crave the novelty of somebody else's house, of furnishings I've never seen, of chairs I've never sat in, and of mirrors in which I've never seen myself, I must have a favorite cup. Otherwise I float around like a Chagall lady, not quite grounded.

We search out the bathrooms, American in their style and efficiency. The house has that marvelous, slightly ruined French look on the outside, but it's very up to date on the inside, no doubt due to the fact that it is owned by Americans. Everything works. The faucets dispense water in a downward direction. The sheets are soft, the water pressure hard, the towels thirsty. The downstairs powder room contains a rustic French basket full of English-language magazines dedicated to French décor.

When you open the drawer in the front hall table, you find all the conveniences of home: batteries, flashlights, scissors, candle stubs, lighters, rubber bands, take-out menus, Post-it notes, and twisties. There's even an English-speaking washer *and* a dryer. There's also a clothesline in the backyard near the fig tree, but sometimes I succumb to using the dryer. We like this house. She will serve us well, but she will seduce and spoil us with her promiscuous Franco-American ways.

The house has her secret places. In the nineteenth and twentieth century, the bottom floor of the newer part of the house served as a communal bakery. People, like us, lived above the store. Determined to find evidence of the bakery, I'm in my best Nancy Drew mode, flashlight in hand. We push through a door under the stairway, grope around for the light switch, and find ourselves in a concrete dungeon-like space that contains nothing more than cleaning supplies. We are disappointed until we find a hole in the wall about the size of a pizza oven. Since there's no one around to contradict us, we declare the laundry room the long-lost bakery. We are ridiculously excited; you'd think we'd discovered the Ark of the Covenant.

In a week or so, we will meet our next-door neighbor, a human sundial who loves to sit outside his house, moving his chair incrementally to follow the light. He remembers that his mother would give him some dough shaped into a loaf to take to the communal bakery on his way to school, with instructions to retrieve the baked loaf on his way home.

After the introductions, we begin to unpack. We fill the armoires, bureaus, and closets with our clothing, the bathroom with our toothbrushes, shampoos, prescription drugs, and other hygienic impedimenta, arranged on "his" or "her" side of the sink.

Then we make a list, locate the nearest supermarket, go shopping, and fill the refrigerator. That accomplished, we spend the requisite three days overcoming jet lag and the *il ne marche pas* parade of computer problems.

NOSTALGIA FOR A LIFE WE NEVER LIVED

After the isolation of Saumane, we have chosen to live in the midst of a village, and the center of Goult offers a lot of midst. Our house is situated, literally, on the square, Place de la Libération, which doubles as a parking lot. A large obelisk stands in the center of the square, a memorial to the soldiers from Goult who died in both world wars. *"Aux enfants de Goult, morts pour La Patrie,"* it reads, and lists the names of all who died, including the names of three Jews *"morts en déportation."*

The twelfth-century medieval church of St. Sébastien stands directly across the square from our house. A larger-than-life-sized sculpture of Jesus on the cross stands diagonally across from the church, at the far corner of the parking lot, just to the right of our doorway.

Persian rug makers used to include a flaw in each of their carpets so that they would not offend God with perfection. I like to think that in medieval times, the bells in the church steeple summoned the workers from the vineyards and fields to their homes, or to the church for vespers, or sounded the dinner and bedtime hours. However, as we are about to learn, the bells of Goult's church, a mere stone's throw from our house, never stop. There is no hunchback at our Notre Dame. If there were, he might have been given the nights off. But no; these bells are set on automatic, 24-7. The chimes are heavenly and authentically informative, if insistent, during the day, when they are set to bong every hour, then two minutes after the hour, in case you need a nudge, and once again at the half hour. But all night long, they are the hammers of hell. First we try earplugs. Then we move on to gateway drugs.

All the commercial enterprises we could wish for are within a few steps of our front door—a *boulangerie-pâtissererie,* a grocery store, two thriving butcher shops, improbably located side by side, one restaurant, and, of course, Le Café de la Poste, which still serves a lemonade that is the real thing, *citron pressé,* so painfully sour that I might as well be drinking alum. Still, in an effort to be French, I order it twice before giving up and switching to Diet Coke. "Co-ca Dee-et," is all you have to say, and one appears. The Académie Française, the protectors of the purity of the French language, must have been very *désoles* when they had to add Co-ca Dee-et to their list of loathed *Franglais* words like *"le hot dog"* and *"le weekend"* that are invading the language like kudzu.

Acceptance as a regular at the local café is the *sine qua non* of feeling French. In L'Isle sur la Sorgue, we were known at La Bellevue. In Goult, we might as well be invisible. Nobody will pay attention to me at Café de La Poste, except for the waiter who must. At least three times a week, after saying *"Bonjour, Monsieur,"* I buy two newspapers, the *International Herald Tribune* and the regional paper, *La Provence,* from the man behind the counter. In an effort to elicit a response, I explain to him in my best French that "One is for reading; the other is for understanding." I think I'm charming. He doesn't crack a smile. He deals a severe blow to my self-esteem as well as to my earnest pretentions.

We look forward to the three-day Fête de Votive de St. Eustache, the annual celebration honoring Goult's patron saint. The event will take place in La Place de la Liberation. Remembering the folksy potluck music festival, the welcoming Feerie Nautique, the fascinating festival of dry stone, and the stirring *fêtes des nego-chin*, we are looking forward to what we are sure will be a celebration of all that is essentially Provençal. There *is* a *boules* competition, but otherwise, for three solid days, we will witness a totally sleazy American carnival, a desecration of all we hold dear as French: good taste and a reverence for tradition. We will be asked to move our car. Huge vans will take over the village square cum parking lot. Workers will string up lights, set up a large dancing stage, a shooting gallery, a carousel, bumper cars, electronic beepers, canned music, and a hundred-foot by twenty-foot mural of a cabaret, featuring the torsos of naked women, their rosy nipples pointing right across the square at the statue of Jesus. What did we expect? Grape-stomping competitions? Olive pressing? Honey harvesting? Medieval Provençal dancers dressed in aprons and wooden clogs?

I suspect that people like me, who are drawn to fantasy, tend to be naive and maybe a bit literal. My grade-school child still imagines her picture book of "cultures from around the world." My grown-up knows better, yet she hopes that Hans Brinker still skates on a frozen canal in the Netherlands, which people used to call Holland. I want to believe that if I go to Japan, I will see men in long pigtails with their arms tucked halfway up their droopy, dragon-decorated, silk sleeves. A native Congolese should be wearing a loincloth and paddling a dug-out canoe. He should not be wearing a Gap T-shirt and plastic flip-flops. He should not be selling trinkets to tourists. He should not take credit cards. And rosy nipples should not be eyeing Christ from across the square.

The Geriatric Tour de France

Larry and I share two habitual activities that we bring with us to Provence: we love to swim and ride bikes. I am most at peace when I am in motion. I suspect Larry is, too. Others sit cross-legged to meditate; we stroke, kick, and pedal. I get genuine pleasure from working my body. Larry calls me "Little Endorphin Annie." In this respect, I am more like my aunt Lily, the serial monogamist who, born before women were meant to exercise or play sports, sought and found the physical workout she craved in sex and, when men were scarce, which was rarely, by rearranging large items of furniture in her living room.

Swimming in Provence is one way we make the Vaucluse our own. Early in our first stay in Saumane, we found a lovely outdoor pool in the Centre Sportif in the nearby town of Pernes les Fontaines, and we've been visiting it ever since. It's too far to bike, so we drive. Taking the plunge for the first time turned out to be more than metaphoric. How much to pay, where to change, where to shower—all matters we take for granted at the YMCA—required us to compose various tortured questions. Between the two of us, we understood the answers. We paid the one euro fee and found our way to the *vestiaire*, where we changed our clothes, he with the *hommes*, me with the *dames*. Then it was on to the *douche*. Standing on a concrete floor in three-sided cubicle, we showered by pushing a chrome button under a metered shower. It was déjà vu all over again.

Under less than ideal conditions, we are the best of sports. We see inconvenience, disappointment, disgrace, and even fear as challenges to which we must rise and, having risen, occasions to celebrate. At least so far we do.

Once in the pool, goggled, capped, and nearly naked, sharing lanes, and swimming laps along with the other swimmers, our mouths in use only to breathe, not to mangle the French language, we are as fully French as we will ever be. When our regular pool closes in mid-September, we find an indoor public pool in Carpentras. It's a rough place, full of hardscrabble, adolescent boys who bray and push and don't stay within the lane markers. Away from our privileged, genteel village life, we get a stiff dose of urban Provençal reality. Larry gets an earache.

Finding an ear, nose, and throat doctor is as challenging as fixing a broken glass refrigerator shelf was on our first day in Saumane. We follow the usual drill: first the dictionary where we learn that the word for ear infection is *otite*, and then on to the yellow pages to find *un oto-rhino-gorge médecin*. We could have saved ourselves the trouble had we bothered to call Ellen. Later she tells us that the names and telephone numbers of the doctors who are on call on any particular day are listed in the local newspaper.

Larry leaves the doctor's office with three prescriptions, which, when filled, cost less than eleven euros. The whole deal, the doctor and three medications, costs the equivalent of fifteen dollars. I'm trying to figure out what's so bad about socialism. Larry also reports that when the doctor aspirated the gunk out of his ear, he said, *"Oh là là."* It turns out the French really do say that.

Desperate for a swim, we search our map for blobs of blue that indicate what we hope are lakes, hop into the car, and hunt them down. Too often they are reservoirs posted with an unfriendly sign, *"Baignade Interdite."* No swimming. We persist. Our determined pursuit takes us almost two hours south of home, to the Camargue region, famous for its bulls and wild horses. The wild horses are exciting. Even when standing still, they seem poised for action. The bulls are only dark smudges against the flat landscape, too far away to enjoy. The terrain is flat and swampy—gorgeously swampy—full of reeds, grasses, egrets, and pink flamingoes, the prima ballerinas of birds.

We head toward the sea and the town of Saintes-Maries de la Mer, which, were it not for an imposing medieval hulk of a church and the fact that this is where the gypsies hold their annual convention, would be little more than a miniature Atlantic City. There are lots of people milling about the strip of stalls on the boardwalk, ordering fast food, hoisting their children onto the carousel horses, and buying tickets to bullfights. Nobody is swimming.

There's no place we can find to change into our swimsuits, so we perform the necessary towel-draped contortions in the car and walk toward the water. We see a fisherman casting his line from a nearby jetty. It's our lucky cognate day when we ask him if there's *un courant dangereux*. There isn't. Half-nude, in this strange landscape, at the edge of Provence, facing a brand-new sea, I feel afraid. I extend a toe. Not too cold. We walk in. The French water closes around and holds us. We are in our element.

A two-hour-long drive, however, is a bit much for a swim, so we give up our quest for water and switch to biking. Our appreciation of the beauty of Provence exists in inverse relationship to the speed with which we travel through it, which is yet another reason why we like to ride our bikes whenever we're able. We miss more when we're driving. Biking slows us down. We pay attention.

There is nothing flimsy about the landscape of Provence. The sun is strong, the sky is a sharp blue, the ubiquitous stone walls are mottled green, white, and black with lichen. The furrows in the fallow fields are stern, and the turned, dry clods of earth are hard. Where there is vegetation on the nearby hills, it is silvery green, but for the most part, these hills are made of sedimentary limestone rock, exposed and raked into horizontal striations weathered smooth by eons of wind and water.

In Saumane, when we first started biking, we pedaled up and down rue de l'Eglise. We wobbled a bit, but then we gained confidence. If we were to go anywhere at all, we had to tackle what must be a one-mile, ninety-degree, precipitous plummet. We gathered up our nerve, fastened our helmets, and flew downhill, squeezing our hand brakes fiercely in a desperate attempt to stay in control. Now, in this our third season, we take the hill leading down from Goult with greater calm.

Once down the hill, we regroup and head out on flatter terrain. We revel in the sheer physical joy of the act, riding in the slipstream of our own childhoods. We are innocent of the ways of the world in which we find ourselves. Everything is a challenge, much the way learning to speak, read, cross the street, make friends, and jump double dutch were the challenges of our childhoods. And because that is the case, we feel inordinately delighted when we meet these challenges. Achievement, I'm convinced, is a crucial element of happiness. Being here, away from our real home and our real lives, we tap into that part of ourselves that is fresh, impressionable, and untried.

This second childhood of ours has other benefits. Sometimes, like children at play, we lose all sense of time. We are suffused with pure awareness, unsullied by self-consciousness. In our stressful adult lives, we're always trying to beat the clock. By contrast, time stands still for children; it's always now o'clock.

During our two months in Saumane, we limited our bike trips to nearby towns, favoring the not so *perché* over the very *perché*. A favorite destination was the pretty, popular town of

Fontaine de Vaucluse. With the hill behind us, we relax and pedal slowly on the flat road beneath a Roman aqueduct and under a bower made by the one-hundred-foot-high, broad-leafed foliage of plane trees. Some sources credit Napoléon with planting these relatives of the sycamore to protect his marching troops from the Provençal sun. If so, they could be two hundred years old. Planted at even intervals on both sides of many a roadway along the "route Napoléon," plane trees are as emblematically Provençal as fields of lavender and sunflowers. They dapple the road with patterns of light and shade. Each time I pedal through these majestic archways, my heart melts. If it is true that one passes through a tunnel at the moment of death, I hope it's this one. It would be a nice introduction to heaven, or wherever.

Unfortunately, these beautiful trees are doomed. They have been infected by an unremitting, killing fungus, thought to have been introduced to the region near the end of the Second World War by American wooden ammunitions boxes that were harboring this virulent blight. Infected trees are cut into pieces and burned on pyres in an effort to retard the demise of those that still stand. Happily, there is an effort underway to replace these doomed giants with an infection-resistant variety. Wait a hundred years or so and they'll be back.

Fontaine de Vaucluse becomes a regular destination. We like to walk through the prehistoric town to the deep cavern that is the source of the Sorgue, so deep that even Jacques Cousteau couldn't get to the bottom of it. On our first visit, we were surprised to see that this very French town is dominated by a museum devoted to the memory of Petrarch, the famous fourteenth-century Italian scholar, poet, humanist, and quite possibly the champion of unrequited infatuation. He is best known for the 366 poems he wrote over a period of twenty-one years to a young beauty named Laura.

Scholars differ as to whether Laura actually existed, but those who believe she did say Petrarch fell in love when he caught his first and last sight of her in a church in Avignon. Laura, assuming she was real, lived in the town of Noves, which may explain why Petrarch chose an ex-pat life in nearby Fontaine, where he lived for years in a house he built on the banks of the river. Maybe there was a Laura. If so, maybe she read his letters, maybe she didn't. One thing is for sure; there's no evidence that she ever wrote back.

After we walk through town, we lean our bikes against the stone wall that separates the narrow main street from the river and order our usual—a banana ice-cream cone for me and an apricot slush for Larry. We turn our backs on the souvenir shops that line the street and train our eyes on the immense waterwheel that creates electricity for the paper factory, and on the kayaks that bob and swivel on the fast-flowing Sorgue. Then we climb back on our bikes and pedal back beneath the aqueduct and under the bower of bliss. Our ultimate goal is to be able to ride all the way home, to the top of Goult—more than a mile—without getting off our bikes two or three times to rest, or, worse yet, having to walk them part of the way uphill.

It doesn't help my morale when a woman who looks older than I, dressed in a faded flowered house dress, her gray hair held in a bun, pedals smoothly past me, without even breathing hard. *"Bon Courage,"* she calls over her shoulder. I, outfitted in my padded Lycra cycling shorts and plastic helmet, don't even have the wind to call back, *"Merci."*

Given our natures, Larry and I compete against the hill and each other to see who can get to the top first without having to get off and rest. That doesn't happen until the last week. We are our own little Tour de France.

At first we used to drive to and from Ulli and Bettina's house from Saumane, but now that we live in Goult, we ride our bikes, a trip of about seven miles. We usually do this on weekends, so that it's possible to pedal there and back and still have enough time to fall into a coma.

We discover a dedicated bike path that starts near Goult and ends in Apt, just a mile or so beyond Perrotet. Once we streak down our hill, we walk our bikes across the treacherously trafficked highway.

Then we take a left onto a narrow, flat, paved road where a rural world of colorful wonders awaits us. We pedal past orange pumpkin fields, wild bouquets of Queen Anne's lace, broom, and pale blue morning glories adorning sagging wire fences. Our path takes us through vineyards abundant with ripening clusters of purple grapes, under stone bridges, and alongside trailer encampments festooned with laundry, where gypsy children and their dogs run wild. We relish the occasional buff-colored, sternly rectangular, plaster-covered stone farmhouses. If the plaster has fallen off here and there, exposing the continent-like shapes of the ancient stonework beneath, and if their once colorful shutters are faded to chalky pastel by years of blazing sunlight, so much the better. We love a ruin.

The most thrilling part of the trip is traversing Le Pont Julien, named after *that* Julien, Julius Caesar. It is a one-lane, two-thousand-year-old, triple-arched Roman bridge in such perfect condition that it's still in use, although cars and bikes must wait their turns at each end to traverse it single file. It will take a few trips over Le Pont Julien before we even begin to get bored with the idea that eons ago, Roman legions in chariots passed this way. We exit the bike path at Perrotet, walk our bikes once more across the highway, and pedal a kilometer or so to Ulli and Bettina's where we wash up and watch our friends put the finishing touches on what the French call lunch and we call a feast.

We start with a kir *apéritif* and hors d'oeuvre of olives and *saucisson*. Then comes a fish course, served with a vegetable, then a goat cheese quiche, then a salad made with arugula and strawberries, after which they serve the requisite cheese plate and finally a chocolate mousse. All the while we're slowly but surely drinking our way through two bottles of light rosé.

Our lunch with Ulli and Bettina has taken at least two hours to consume, not so much because it is so bountiful—although there is a natural pause between courses that slows the process down—but because we take our time. Even for would-be Provençaux, eating is one of the best reasons for being alive.

It is when we are with Ulli and Bettina that we are the most conscious of the difference between pretending and intending to be French. Even so, I sometimes lose my grip on fantasy and trespass in the dangerous territory of reality.

"We could do what they have done," I say to Larry, after a visit to their tiny, huggable house. "We could retire. We could be *a la retraite.* We could sell our house and buy a little place in Provence. In six months, we'd be speaking decent French. You could stop being a lawyer. You could calm down. You could cook organ meats. You could experiment with watercolors. Let's have one more grand adventure. Why not? C'mon. There's nothing to stop us."

"Nothing," says Larry, "except our friends, our house, which is twice the size of the lamb shed, the YMCA pool, the gym, and the library. Plus, you'd have to find an internist, an allergist, a dentist, a gynecologist, a psychopharmacologist, and we're much too old, we don't have the nerve, and we'd run out of money."

We take turns going sane. This time it was his turn.

A TYPE A COUPLE IN A TYPE B WORLD

In class, we listen to a recording by the late Fernandel, himself a Provençal, singing a Provençal song. The first line of each stanza begins, *"Aujourd'hui peut-être, ou plutôt demain,"* (maybe today, or better yet tomorrow) the Provençal equivalent of *mañana*. As the verses go, Fernandel delays cutting off a tree branch that threatens to crash through his roof, puts off harvesting grass to feed his rabbits, and can't even find the wherewithal to make love on his wedding night.

The singer claims he is suffering from *la flemme*, a serious case of lethargy brought on by the intensity of the Provençal sun. While his *flemme* is exaggerated to the point of comedy, it is true that the natives like to take it easy, at least in the warm season, which is when we are there. The heat slows people down. They pace themselves. They stroll. They hang out. They linger. They take their time. They nap.

Like mad dogs and Englishmen, we go out in the midday sun, from one to four o'clock, when all the stores, except the supermarkets, are closed. The natives know the sun will boil your brain, and besides, why not take a little three-hour break? We could go home and study or play Scrabble, or read a book, or even make love. Sometimes we do, but too often our siesta time includes taking a bike ride or food shopping. We may not be tourists, but we tend to move at a touristic pace. Maybe if we knew we were staying longer than a month, we'd slow down a bit, but too often, at the end of the day, we reach for the ibuprofen.

Once in a while, we achieve that coveted phlegmatic state of mind we so admire. We will sit in the salon and read all afternoon. Larry will take his watercolors outdoors and paint village scenes. I find my calm center daily when I write.

Sometimes we take a walk, with no destination in mind. Often, when we're walking in one village or another, Larry will unaccountably come to an abrupt halt, take out his camera, and engage in his own version of time-lapse photography. He is drawn to vintage advertisements that have faded into the plaster walls on which they had been painted decades ago. I would have walked right by without noticing, but now I do. The best ones are so faded that one can't really make out all the letters. Bleached by the sun, abraded by winds and time, their colors retreat into the walls, leaving a beguiling penumbra of their former practical selves. These signs are another way of seeing through time. In this and many other matters aesthetic, I count on Larry to show me what's beautiful.

Often we will drive to the top of Saignon, a very quiet *village perché*. Centuries ago it was a defensive outpost for the nearby town of Apt. Today it is a refuge for the stressed. We sit in the outdoor café on the sun-dappled patio, next to a beautifully time and weather-worn fountain dedicated to Ceres, the goddess of fertility. We each order an Orangina and stare across the patterned Luberon Valley below. Our guidebook describes Saignon as "a typically peaceful village, not demanding of your attention." Exactly.

Mo has told us that she has broken up with Ange. Now she is with Marc. Ulli says that Mo is totally gaga over Marc.

We are eager to meet Mo's new boyfriend, so we invite them to dinner. Marc is a darkly attractive man and, like so many people we meet through Mo, smart and interesting, too.

Larry and I are in hyper-hosting mode. We take turns rushing back and forth into the kitchen, stabbing anxiously at the beef stew, making sure it's tender, loading the coffeepot, deciding not to put the dressing on the salad quite yet, checking the crust on the tomato pie, remembering and then forgetting to put the salt and pepper shakers on the table, and otherwise being our usual, anxious American selves.

When we finally settle down at the table, we shift into conversational mode. We talk, with great enthusiasm, as we often do, about how much we have enjoyed our two previous stays in Provence and how much we love the villages, the people, the language, the aesthetic, and, well, so much that is French.

Marc responds to our proclamations of Francophilia with a question. "What, if any, changes do you want to make to your lives at home as a result of having spent these months in Provence?"

"That's easy," I answer. "We are determined to live more slowly, to relax, to stay longer at the table, not to worry so much." It doesn't occur to me at the time that if we can't relax in Provence, it's unlikely we'll be laid back at home. Maybe that's why Marc is smiling.

BEST FRIENDS

We enjoy a very active social life in Provence, a cat's cradle of interconnectedness, with Mo holding the strings. Much of it takes place at lunchtime when Mo invites her friends to share a meal, to meet us, and to oblige us to speak French to people other than herself. Sometimes they become our friends, at least for the time we are in Provence.

The French have a reputation for being rude and stand-offish. We find no evidence of that stereotype; in fact, we find plenty of evidence that the opposite is true. This friendliness displays itself in many ways. The French literally stand closer to one another than Americans do. After the initial introductory handshake, the triple kiss (or double in Paris) is de rigueur, creating an instant intimacy—a blending of touch and breath—that may be utterly lacking in substance but is nevertheless loaded with good will. Men don't just kiss and hug women they hardly know; they hug and kiss one another.

In America, strangers in an elevator tend to face the doors and ride to their floors in stony silence. In France, they are much more likely to talk to one another. The requisite *"Bonjour, Madame"* or *"Bonjour, Monsieur"* upon entering a store sets the scene for a friendly, if merely commercial, encounter. Even while seated at separate restaurant tables, diners will greet one another upon being seated, and as we have experienced, may even converse table to table during the meal.

The language, too, reflects the French inclination toward affection by the frequent use of diminutives. *Petit* often modifies a French noun to make the object even more endearing. *Un ami* is a friend. *Un petit ami* is a boyfriend, even if he's six feet tall. Similarly, *"un petit restaurant"* designates a positive recommendation, even if the restaurant takes up a city block. There, the waiter will ask if you'd like *"un petit café"* or *"un petit dessert."* It's not accidental that this inclination to minimize mimics the fondness that is lavished on babies and small children who are both *adorable* and *petit*. We become *les petits Américains*.

All this, and more, we figure, inclines the Provençaux to look kindly upon starry-eyed, late middle-aged Francophiles who are eager to speak their language and to blend into their culture. Sometimes we imagine they are thinking (in French), *Look at that adorable old couple. One has to admire them for trying to learn French at their age.*

Or maybe not. Maybe they're just being nice, and it is we who are overreacting to the slightest act of politesse.

At home or away, we are by nature promiscuously friendly. We tend to like at first sight, too often mistaking well-informed people for deep thinkers and the certifiably insane for delightfully eccentric. Still, we must have friends to feel at home. We understand that real friendships take time and a sense of future, neither of which we've got, but we can't afford to let that bother us. We're so busy being nice, and they are so busy being nice back, whether we actually like one another or not is hardly relevant. In reality, it could take a long time to find out that we're not well suited, but since we only have a month, at best, these pretend friendships define superficiality and need not survive the test of time. Here our tendency toward promiscuity serves us well.

If we find ourselves attracted to someone, we simply shortcut the getting to know you part and go directly to best friends. In this respect, we are like our granddaughter Isabelle. She has what she calls her BFF, her best friend forever. She also has a spare BFF in case the first one doesn't work out.

We distinguish among potential friends the same way we distinguish among words in the French language; they're either *faux amis* or *vrais amis*—people with whom we will never get beyond the superficial and people with whom we might. Usually, and not surprisingly, the *faux amis* tend to speak no English. We will do our best to speak with them at lunch. We may run into them at a fête or in the marketplace, but neither of us pursues a relationship. It's not worth the effort. When we pass in the street, we recognize one another with a quick exchange of "*Ça va?*" and keep moving.

Mo's table becomes a proving ground. If we can understand their French, and they can put up with ours, they may turn out to be *vrais amis*. Some of the people we meet invite us to their homes and welcome us warmly. We are often the center of attention. We find ourselves amending our politesse theory to the assumption that they may find us fascinating. Perhaps it's because, in these small towns, everybody knows everybody except us, which, in addition to the fact that we're Americans and friends of Mo's, makes us persons of interest. Or perhaps they are as eager to understand our world as we are theirs. Or maybe Mo pays them.

Mo has invited a distinguished elderly gentleman from Paris to lunch. She prepares us for his visit. We will notice that he wears a medal on his lapel. He is a member of La Legion d'Honneur, indicating that he made a significant contribution to the military or to French culture. His contributions, she tells us, were primarily in the field of history, but his current passion is the preservation of the purity of the French language. He has joined forces with L'Academie Francaise to do battle against the inevitable lethal leakage of what they call *franglais* into the purity of the French language. They get cramps when their countrymen say, "No problem," when they ought be saying, *"Pas de souci."* Ditto for words like "e-mail," "networking," and "chat."

Mo has made a terrible mistake. Did she mean to show us off? She may have thought that Larry and I were ready to converse with a real Parisian, but we are not—so *very* not that after several attempts to understand a single word he mutters, we fall mute.

We pass *le pain*, and the pain, between us. We dab various spreads on crackers. We chew slowly. We twist our napkins one way and then another. We fiddle with the edge of the tablecloth. We avoid eye contact for fear of bursting into the kind of unstoppable, nervous laughter that used to get me sent to the principal's office.

Mo realizes her error and turns her conversational attention to her guest. Their conversation is, not surprisingly, about the French language. Mo commiserates with her guest about how a French tennis player is now often described as *"un tennisman."* She wants the Academy to revive *"joueur de tennis,"* tennis player. The French word didn't need Anglicizing. The French language had a perfectly good word of its own. *Non?*

We understand more when Mo speaks. They are discussing the new, hopeful, and perhaps doomed effort on the part of the Academy to rescue those French words that have become Anglicized. To this end, the Academy has sponsored a competition to translate these errant words into French. Without much success, they have tried to convert "Walkman" to "Baladeur," and "e-mail" to *"courriel."*

At that moment, Larry, the irrepressible, whispers in my ear, "How are they planning to repatriate *le hot dog*? *Le chien chaud*?" This causes both of us to excuse ourselves from the table and rush into a distant room to bang our heads on the wall to cover up the sound of our laughter. Fortunately, Monsieur has fallen asleep.

The outcome is much more pleasant when we are invited to a party at Julie's house. Julie, whom we met briefly at Mo's table, has moved to the countryside outside of Lacoste. She is giving a party and invites us to come along. We have no idea if we want to go, but Mo encourages us. She and Marc will drive us there.

Julie greets us and introduces us to her guests. Again we experience the pleasure of an enthusiastic welcome. Too many of them are named some variant of Marie. Besides me, Mary-Lou, there's Marie Ann and Marie Therese, a just plain Marie, and even a guy named Marius, who's married to Mary Ann. When Larry is introduced to a woman named Laurence, everyone enjoys a big icebreaker of a laugh. A hearty Côtes-du-Rhône conspires with coincidence, and soon conversation is also flowing. The mood is informal. Some people have brought their children to keep Julie's three-year-old boy company. The toddlers lurch about, engaging with guests, speaking better French than we do.

Julie's soirée is an extravaganza of superficial friendliness. In spite of their obvious limitations, superficial friendships have their advantages. Our conversations, such as they are, are fueled by sheer goodwill. For all we know, we could be triple kissing thieves and serial killers. It took us two sojourns in the Vaucluse to figure out that one of our friends is suffering from advanced Alzheimer's.

I would not have thought it possible to be friends with people who cannot speak English, but our relationship with Sylvie and Alain Prétot proves me wrong. Even if we can't finish each other's sentences—sometimes we can't even understand them—there is friendship in smiles, in gestures, in touch, in favors, in offerings of food and drink, in the light in their eyes whenever we meet. Because they live just a few doors away from Mo, we see them often. Sylvie, especially, exudes a sense of warmth and welcome.

An invitation to stop by for a drink turns out to be a full-course dinner. It is her earth-motherly nature to give, and we find her irresistible. In time, as our French improves, we begin to know them both beyond superficial, conversational niceties. Larry finds a cooking companion in Alain. They button themselves into their white chef's jackets—Alain keeps a couple at home—and bond over a vol-au-vent.

The long hours we've spent studying and socializing in Mo's home makes intimacy inevitable, even though she can't speak English, or at least claims she can't. She tries to maintain a certain professionalism and discipline, but because we're in her company so often, there is no way she can isolate us from her private life or she from ours. *Merde* happens. Her washer overflows. She suffers from migraines. She suspects her son is smoking pot. She thinks about retirement. So does Larry. In Provence, he loves painting watercolors. He enjoys reading for hours on end. But, he wonders out loud to Mo, whether he would do that at home if he really retired. I tell Monique about my parents with candor usually reserved for the analytic couch. Mo catalogues the many ways that Ange was a total creep. We never knew him well enough to notice. We arrange for a Franco-American marriage between her first grandchild, Quentin, and Isabelle.

The downside of this relationship is that Mo is less and less our professor and more and more our friend. It is our fault. Mo is eager to teach us the subjunctive mood if we'd let her, but we won't. We would rather become French than learn French. By now, Mo says, we ought to have finished all the tenses, but we have so much fun talking and joking with her in our mediocre French that we often undermine our pursuit of fluency in favor of fun.

When *vrais* are English speakers, the potential for friendship increases. I never expected to make real friends in Provence; the language barrier alone would see to that. But with Ulli and Bettina, there are no barriers, just minor bumps. We've got a leg up, so to speak, since at all times we've got one and a half languages in common. Both Ulli and Bettina speak decent English. When our French fails us, we migrate to English. We talk candidly about everything: what's happening to America, what's wrong with Angela Merkel, where we've traveled before, their intense dislike of Germans, the Muslim headscarf, their sexual histories, our marital problems, their latest tag sale acquisitions, the existence of God, how Ange turned out not to be as nice as he seemed, and why, then, do we suppose that Mo stayed with him for as long as she did. When you can gossip in French, you've arrived.

With Bob and Ellen, we don't even bother to speak French. In fact, the day that Mo introduced me to Ellen at lunch, we automatically retreated from the dining room to the hallway where Mo couldn't hear us, and began to speak mad, passionate English. We are like seatmates on a long airplane trip, throwing conversational caution to the winds. Perhaps that sense of impermanence is why our friendships, as with Ulli and Bettina, happen so quickly and carry such a charge. It is also true that we have been preselected to get along. We already have a lot in common: we are adventurers, we are on foreign soil, and we are all trying to be French.

SOMEONE PUT A BANANA IN MY CHARDONNAY

Petty humiliations happen daily. Usually I am able to accept them as no-pain, no-gain learning experiences. The unpleasant feeling is quickly forgotten, and I switch over to trying to correct and memorize the mispronounced word or other evidences of ignorance. Embarrassment is a great teacher. But when the constantly hovering drone of humiliation bombs on me three times in one day, even Paxil won't help.

Day breaks, spilling a torrent of chilly rain on Provence. Bad weather on this particular day is especially annoying because Mo has decided that we are to visit a vineyard. I put on my raincoat and take a shortcut through the parking lot to the *pâtisserie* to buy two of what has become our favorite treat, a sacristan, a flakey almond pastry sprinkled with confectioner's sugar.

Since I see the baker nearly every morning, I decide to comment on how bad the weather is, how it's raining constantly. It's the French thing to do; the French love to talk about the weather. *"Quel mauvais temps,"* I say. "What terrible weather." *"Il pleure sans cesse."* "It doesn't stop raining." I'm very pleased with myself, so I wonder why she looks at me as if I were nuts.

On my way home, I check my yellow dictionary. The infinitive for rain is *pleuvoir*; the infinitive for cry is *pleurer*. Great! I have told her that I cry constantly.

Next stop on my mortification tour: the vineyard. We are met and escorted around the property by Dominique, a young and gorgeous vintner who, even though she's female, is the personification of one of the most important French traditions ever—winemaking.

In a brief introduction, delivered inside the winery, she explains that her family has been producing wine for hundreds of years, as far back as anyone can remember. It is a foregone conclusion on the part of her parents and relatives that she will inherit the vineyard and become a winemaker. The fact that she is a woman seems to be irrelevant, even when so many business signs read, "Somebody or other and Sons." No doubt, at this very moment, somewhere in California's Napa Valley, a father is grooming his daughter to take charge of the Beaujolais Nouveau. She may be one of the first female American vintners to break the grape ceiling.

Dominique is not resigned to the role of tradition in her life; she embraces it. Her ambitions are defined by the past. I, by contrast, come from a country so young that it hasn't had a chance to accumulate many traditions, and from a family so fractured by divorce or distance that they can't even agree to get together once a year and carve a turkey.

Now it's time to tramp around the vineyard. Dominique's got a supply of one-size-fits-all rubber boots for visitors. It is raining harder than ever. Our boots make raunchy noises as we slog through the sticky mud. Larry, Ulli, and I share an umbrella. I am having a terrible time. It was William James who said you could make yourself feel better by smiling. So far it's not working.

Once back inside the winery, it's time for the wine tasting. My mood improves. Dominique pours us each a glass of wine from a bottle of one of her best Chardonnays. First we have a swishing lesson. I am unable to swish the wine in a circular motion in the glass. Larry is instantly expert. So is Ulli. Mo, of course, is swishing just fine. She was probably born knowing how, just as she was born knowing how to tie a scarf. I am so determined to master swishing that I create a kind of storm at sea as waves of wine splash over the rim of my glass and drip down my hand. I have never been *so not French*.

Next we are instructed to sniff the wine to detect its "nose." I've never understood that little affectation. *I'm* the one with the nose. *It's* the one with the smell. I raise my glass and sniff. It smells like wine to me, but since I know that's not the answer, I know to keep my nose down and my mouth shut.

When it's time to taste, my luck changes.

"I detect a hint of banana," I say. I really do taste banana. I'm not making it up.

"Extraordinare!" Dominique declares. *"Incroyable!"* Even Larry and Monique are impressed by how natively French and subtle my taste buds are. Dominique affirms that there are, indeed, notes of banana in this Chardonnay. And then I blow

it by asking at what point in the process do they mix in the bananas. Everyone stares as me in total disbelief. That's my morning.

My afternoon is worse. Now it's raining harder, but even so I decide to try to save the day. There's an exercise class that's held in the church basement across the parking lot, and exercise always makes me feel better. Plus, an exercise class offers an excellent opportunity to insinuate myself into village life. I look forward to meeting some local women; surely they'd want to chat with this American stranger in their midst. I slip into the class, clutching my mat. Nobody even acknowledges me with a bonjour. I take my place and try to follow the directions barked out by the leader. *"Baissez votre bassin!"* she commands. I have no idea what she wants of me, except that *votre* means "your." I know that the lake in the center of L'Isle sur la Sorgue is called a *bassin,* but that gets me nowhere. *Baisser,* as far as I know, means to kiss, but surely she does not want me to kiss my lake. The instructor, in utter disgust, marches over to my nicely arched body and pushes on my stomach, forcing me to lower my pelvis. After class, I roll up my mat—nobody says *à bientôt*—and head home.

I look up the pertinent words in the dictionary. *La bise* means a kiss. *Le bisou* is a social kiss, the kind you plant three times on people's cheeks when saying hello or goodbye. *Le baiser* is a passionate kiss, as between lovers. Or at least it used to be. The B-word is now synonymous with the F-word, so if you want to stay on the safe side of sex, use *embrasser*, which still means "to kiss."

I run my finger down the page a little further and learn that *baisser*, with two s's means "to lower or go down." So *that's* what she meant. I should lower something, but what? In the treacherous French language, *bassin* means pelvis as well as lake. Now I get it. She wanted me to lower my pelvis. I will suffer one more humiliation with the deadly *baisser/baiser* homonyms. Flying home that year, the French flight attendant will roar with laughter when I ask her if my seat goes down on itself.

PROVENCE IN A SUITCASE

We can tell that our month in Goult is coming to an end; the digital device on the dashboard of our car blinks away the days, nearing the thirty days that September hath. My Monday through Sunday pill dispensers are running low; the toothpaste tube is rolled to the max. We embark on a long goodbye.

When I was a kid, whenever we went on a trip, I would hang out of the window as my father backed the DeSoto out of the driveway and wave goodbye to everything in sight. "Goodbye, house! Goodbye, lawn! Goodbye, mailbox! Goodbye, driveway!" I'd keep it up all the way to "Goodbye, neighborhood!" I reenact the same ritual when leaving Provence, especially when it comes to people.

We "goodbye" everyone we know—René, Danielle, Catherine, Yves, Alain, Sylvie. We go to our last class with Monique and bid her a tearful goodbye.

After class we go out for a farewell dinner with Ulli and Bettina. They take this occasion to announce that they are planning to take a trip to New York City and the New England states during the coming year. Of course they'll be staying with us as a part of their trip. We're delighted. It's not goodbye; it's *à bientôt*.

We are in a totem-toting mood. We want to bring Provence home with us. I must buy French spiral notebooks, the kind with grids, even though they look identical to American notebooks. I hoard French toothbrushes. They're just enough different from American ones that they'll remind me at least twice a day of my love for Provence. I also must import those flat, little, yellow cellulose sponges that come in net bags and swell to normal sponge size when submerged in water, even though, a few days later, when I get home, I will find them in Trader Joe's. Nor are we beyond smuggling. We buy four bottles of our favorite prepared vinaigrette and a long string of figatelli, wrapped multiple times to hold in its gamey aroma.

Most unbelievably, Larry wants to buy a pocketbook, the kind that French businessmen carry. After a month of seeing how normal it is for Frenchmen to carry pocketbooks, he is ready to take the plunge. We linger for nearly an hour in a men's leather store while Larry explores various pocketbooks' inner and outer features, all the while talking himself into the virtues of having all his important stuff easily accessible and organized in one place, instead of rattling around in his pants and jacket pockets.

He buys one. Such is the power of Larry's desire to be French that he actually believes that he is going to carry a pocketbook. Larry? I don't think so, and I am right. The bag hangs, unused, on a hook in his closet, next to the beret he bought the year before.

Our actual trip home, like all our returns from Provence, whether from Nice or Paris, seems agonizingly endless. I do in-seat isometrics. I read. I make notes to myself, which, if implemented, would improve my life. Some people do these life assessments at the new year. I find that I get the best view of my life from a perspective of thirty-six thousand feet, and the best ideas of how to improve it. I will get up earlier. I will remember to defrost dinner in the morning, so I won't have to melt it in the microwave at night. I will join a French conversation class. I will find time to relax and read in the afternoons instead of waiting until bedtime when I'm too tired. I will watch less television. I will use the living room more. I will rid my closet of every item of clothing that I haven't worn in two years and take it to Goodwill. I will eat less meat. I will be a nicer person. Unfortunately, as I learn over and over again, my resolutions don't adapt well at ground level.

I watch the movie *North by Northwest* twice. I obsessively return to the airline channel that displays the progress of our tiny black plane as it moves glacially along its trajectory from

London, across the Atlantic, to New York's JFK. Whenever I check our progress, the icon seems stubbornly frozen, like a faulty computer cursor, over Nova Scotia. Nevertheless, the endless agony of going home won't stop us from returning next year. Soon the bad travel memory will fade into the kind of dumb obscurity usually reserved for childbirth.

In the Fourth Place

Living Sideways

The Vaucluse is becoming our home away from home. After three years, the thrill of the new has morphed into the comfort, the pleasure, and sometimes even the boredom of the familiar. It was inevitable. My father was right. The butler no longer relishes the fantasy of presiding over a well-run household. On the other hand, that doesn't mean he isn't enjoying the reality.

We know the drill. We buy our plane tickets. We land in de Gaulle, hop on the fast train to Avignon, sit in the right seats, pick up the rental car, and navigate the rotaries like pros. We head off in *toutes directions* toward L'Isle sur la Sorgue, past towns whose names we know by heart, drugstores where we've filled prescriptions, stands of plane trees, restaurants where we've eaten more than once, and ATMs where we've turned credit cards into euros. Familiarity doesn't breed contempt; it breeds familiarity. It's good to be almost home.

We're headed for a different medieval house in a different medieval town near the top of yet another charming hilltop village, Bonnieux, population 1,408, not counting us. A new house is the novelty on which we thrive. It challenges us to make ourselves at home. The same is true for a change of town. We like our address—rue Voltaire. As was the case with Goult, our house is in the center of town but far enough away from the town's two churches to allow for an uninterrupted night's sleep.

Instructions from the house's American owner advise us to park our car in the street below, across from the twelfth-century ramparts. We soon find out that the ramparts also serve as the foundation of our terrace. They're *our* ramparts! We are off to a very good start.

We asked Ulli and Bettina to check out the house before we signed the rental contact, but in spite of several drives through Bonnieux searching for rue Voltaire, they had been unable to locate it. Now we know why. The so-called street leading to our front door is narrow, unmarked, one way, and so steep that one could easily assume it's a driveway. To approach our front door, one must angle one's body forward, like Miss Clavel from Ludwig Bemelman's *Madeleine*.

No one in their right mind would rent a house most easily approached on all fours, but we are not in our right minds. We are pretending to be French. The cant of our street will also have the virtue of canceling out my caloric intake of sacristans and croissants even before I reach the best *pâtisserie* in town, which, we will soon learn, is even further up the hill.

Rue Voltaire isn't the only ridiculously steep road in town. There's the hill that leads to the town's most famous landmark, the well-named twelfth-century High Church, La Haute Eglise, which sits defiantly at the top of eighty-six steps, testing the devotion of the faithful. In medieval times, the locals, charged with carrying the coffins to the church, used to complain that the dead buried the living.

Larry and I arrive at our rental home, panting and laughing. We stand askew, our hands planted on our hips for balance. Does somebody else's life get better than this?

Yes it does. We will spend the next month living in a view. When Vincent, the caretaker, opens the door, our eyes are ineluctably drawn right through the house to the panorama below. We cross the living room and open the French doors— what else?—and step onto a very large stone patio, twice as wide as it is deep, bordered by the rampart. Our eyes widen at the sight that lies below: first the cockeyed geometry of the orange tile roofs; then the wide and deep Luberon valley—its towns, its patchwork of farms, its church spires, its miniature roads and tiny cars. We identify Goult, our last hilltop hometown, just across the highway and a bit to the east. There's the Pierre Cardin-branded ancient town of Lacoste, easily recognized by the crenellated de Sade castle where, in the eighteenth century, the Marquis spent his adult years, when he wasn't in jail or an asylum for the insane. And that's definitely ochre-colored Rousillon, and Apt even further to the east. On a clear day, we can see Mont Ventoux.

To the extent possible, we will live our daily lives on this terrace. Larry, wearing a floppy white canvas hat, will paint the rooftops and the houses below, angling his watercolor pad on the rampart's rough edge. Or, if I'm not around, he'll steal a smoke. We'll play Scrabble on the large, round metal table, or we'll eat, or read, or stare into space. Is it possible that we have caught a touch of *la flemme*? Are we relaxing?Perhaps we're turning into lowercase type a's.

Nighttime on the patio is even better. The lights of the towns below us will begin to turn on, creating grids, star shapes, and arabesques of illumination. At exactly 9:06 the lights of the castle go on—not all at once but gradually, theatrically. It takes several seconds for the castle to emerge from the dark in all its crenellated glory. Why 9:06 p.m. instead of 9:00 p.m. we can't imagine. We ask. Nobody knows for sure, but a friend blames the lag time on the new sluggish, energy-saving fluorescent lighting that, by law, has replaced incandescent bulbs. We, of course, were hoping for a more romantic explanation. Still, whenever we are at home, we will watch the clock and make sure we're on the terrace in our places to watch the lights brighten.

Although we didn't bother to notice the interior of the house when we made a beeline for the patio, it will turn out to be almost as extraordinary as the view. When we step from the patio into the salon and refocus our eyes, there, on the coffee table, in front of the fireplace, is a welcoming vase of sunflowers from Vincent and a bowlful of home-grown organic tomatoes from Vincent's father. They live in the house next door. We value this welcoming neighborliness. Larry will quickly respond with his version of peasant soup, which M. Giles's father will pronounce "the best he's ever eaten," thereby initiating a month-long potlatch of culinary exchanges.

Clearly, the house has been added to over the centuries. The kitchen is located two steps down from the salon. It's small but large enough to cook up some boiling oil to throw over the ramparts. Larry must duck down in order not to hit his head. People were smaller in the thirteenth century. We figure such historic legitimacy is worth a few cracks on the head.

I look under the sink and attempt to translate the small print on the mysterious plastic bottles. No matter which house we live in, the owners stock different brands of cleansers. They're for washing—but what? The label on one box reads *Le Chat*. It can't be cat detergent. I read the directions but am still unsure, due to my ignorance of a word or two. Place in the *what*? Turn dial on *what* and wait for *what*? It's either dishwashing or laundry detergent. A picture of a T-shirt, nearly concealed by the price sticker, solves that problem. After three seasons in Provence, I still have to rely on rebus.

A tower near the entrance to the kitchen and just off the salon leads by way of a daunting spiral staircase to the bedroom floors above. I hug the walls, mounting the isosceles-shaped stone steps, wide at one end and narrow at the other, with extreme caution. If a twenty-first-century preosteoporotic person were to fall, her bones might crumble like halva. That can't have worried women in the thirteenth century since most people didn't live long enough to develop osteoporosis. They didn't know about fitness or weight-bearing activities either, unless it was a hoisting a load of firewood or swinging a battle-ax. This is the oldest house we've ever lived in. Age is authenticity to us. More than any of the other centuries-old houses we've rented, this one gives us the illusion that we are living in a time we never knew.

We like Bonnieux's dark and bloody past. From Neolithic times until the sixteenth century, inhabitants of *villages perchés* like Bonnieux were perched for defensive purposes, first to fight off the various raids and sieges by Franks, Arabs, and Berbers, kicking up limestone dust in the valley below. In Roman times, Bonnieux, the largest hill town in the area, saw the worst of these sieges due to its strategic location on the route between two popular Roman destinations, Cadiz and Milan. The town took such a beating from rival, warring tribes that in the twelfth century it was moved further up the hill, and ramparts were built for extra protection. Our ramparts. These villages were not located on the tops of hills so that centuries later tourists could enjoy their charms, or so that Larry and I could climb onto our bikes and compete to see who could get to the top first.

By the sixteenth century, most of the town's inhabitants were Catholic, many of them wealthy bishops who lived in mansions. This situation so infuriated the less wealthy Huguenots in the neighborhood—later known as Protestants—that they laid siege to Bonnieux, killing three thousand of its four thousand citizens. The town has never recovered its population.

We do not dwell on the negatives of medieval times, when life was "nasty, brutish, and short," even before Hobbes said so. Our teeth would be rotten or gone altogether, my hair would be white, and, with a life expectancy in the thirties, we'd both be dead by now, most likely of the bubonic plague. Medieval is a nice place to visit, but you wouldn't want to live there.

Vincent Giles is more than a good neighbor and caretaker. He rents the Neolithic cave across the street, where he sells antiques. In between waiting on customers, he sits on a tiny wooden chair, which wobbles a bit on the uneven limestone cavern floor. Small antique items—silver spoons, bowls, candlesticks—rest on centuries-smoothed ledges dug into the cave walls.

Le Fournil, the restaurant at the bottom of our hill, where we will dine often and happily, is also set into a natural troglodyte cave, which formerly served as the village bakery. These caves are blatant evidence that the earliest people, before there was a Provence or a France for that matter, lived in these caves.

There's an active street life just outside our door. Weddings march by on their way to the church. Shoppers duck in and out of Vincent's antiques cave. Friends stop to chat. Others trudge by at a slant, carrying groceries from the convenience store at the bottom of the hill. Tourists pause in front of our house, which is about halfway up the hill, to catch their breath. Attracted by the view, they peer shamelessly into our front windows. One exhausted woman plops herself down on our doorstep and calls for help. We lift her up and haul her in for a glass of water.

These villages seem like natural communities to us. I understand that I'm in danger of naïveté and that even as I sing its praises, village life in the Vaucluse is on the way out. Here the old and the new mix uneasily. The ringtones of cell phones compete with bongs of church bells; plumbing pipes that run down the outsides of thirteenth-century homes disperse wastewater from twenty-first-century bathrooms. People park their cars in old stables. Some streets are simply too narrow to drive down, but the government doesn't respond by seizing the houses on one side or the other by eminent domain to widen the roadways. If they did, these towns would lose the aesthetic authenticity and the richness of history the French, the tourists, and we so cherish.

M. Giles, the father, and his retired cronies make a daylong occupation of leaning against the doorway of their house next door, shooting the *merde.* There they stand at a constant tilt, one foot on the up side of the street, the other anchored on the down side. If Darwinian adaptation worked at warp speed, these guys would have developed one long and one short leg, but so far they haven't mutated.

Housewives call to one another from window to window across the narrow street. To find community in my suburban hometown, people have to get in their cars and drive somewhere to something organized—a library activity, or the women's club, a bridge game, a reading group, or the senior center. It's hard to imagine an old man or woman being lonely in Bonnieux, as long as they are still able to lean against a wall.

I have begun to worry about my old age. So have my friends. We fear the loss of our spouses. We fear loneliness, dependence, and declining health. We don't want to be a burden to our children, although, only God knows why; they've been a burden to us.

We've had lots of conversations about how we might live communally. We'd sell our houses. Maybe we'd buy an abandoned summer camp. We'd all share a kitchen and cook together. We'd take care of one another. Those of us who could still walk would push the wheelchairs of those who couldn't.

The discussions invariably break down. Pool our money? Share a bathroom? Live in Florida? Why not the Berkshires?

Americans are individualists; the French not so much. When the time comes, we'll probably all end up in what Larry calls "insistent living." The French have developed their own version of continuing care, much of it government funded, but at least in villages like Bonnieux, it is still common for elderly parents to be cared for by their children. Apparently, they're not a burden, at least not yet.

THE MORE THINGS CHANGE, THE MORE THEY'RE DIFFERENT

Our first act after unpacking is a phone call to Ulli and Bettina to invite them to dinner. We are eager to see them. We last saw them when they visited us in the wintertime on their tour of

New England. Even though their jobs didn't allow them much spare money, the euro was still high against the dollar; they couldn't resist the temptation. Besides, it was Bettina's fortieth birthday, and Ulli had never been to the United States. Bettina was eager to show her around. The climax of their trip would be a side trip to New York City where Ulli was determined to sample American jazz. Their spirits were high, or at least we thought they were. We had had a wonderful time in their company. When they headed north toward Boston, Lexington, and Concord to visit American revolutionary sites, we sent them off with a bottle of champagne, since they'd be in Boston on Bettina's birthday.

Ulli answers the phone and accepts the invitation. We instruct her to park her car at the bottom of the hill and meet us at Le Fournil. At the appointed hour, we go to greet Ulli and Bettina and find only Ulli. They have broken up. Ulli tells us that Bettina has fallen in love with another woman who is married and has three children.

"I was happy with Bettina," Ulli tells us over dinner at Le Fournil. "I thought Bettina was happy with me. I thought we'd be together for a lifetime." Ulli cried for a few days, she allows, but now she has pulled herself together. Her French is good enough so that she has secured a position working with handicapped children in the very same facility where Bettina works. In fact, Bettina helped Ulli get her job.

Why isn't she carrying on as I would? How could Bettina be so unkind, so fickle? How could Bettina commit to a lifetime with Ulli, move with her to a foreign land, buy a house, and then, after only two years, leave Ulli in the lurch? I am prepared to share my outrage with Ulli, but she's having none of it. Is she already that French, all that *c'est la vie?* Or maybe her stoicism is leftover Teutonic.

Throughout the rest of the month, Ulli will invite Bettina to dinner whenever she invites us, but Bettina will always find an excuse to refuse. Perhaps she is embarrassed. Perhaps she finds it impossibly awkward to mix her old life with us with her new life and new love. Perhaps we do, too, since we never ask Ulli for Bettina's current phone number. We never see Bettina again, and we miss her.

Happily, our friendship with Ulli will deepen. She introduces us to the special-needs adults with whom she works. She has joined a chorus. We go to hear her sing. After two years in Provence, she seems fully integrated in the life of the region.

We attend a concert of Haydn chorales together in the church in L'Isle along with her friend Dominique. After the concert, Dominique invites us back to her house in L'Isle for what she calls a snack. Do all fully employed French women have leftovers in their refrigerators that are the equivalent of a first-class, three-course meal? Out come a variety of *pâtés,* a rice salad, and an apricot *tarte.* Surprise me at my house, and you'd be lucky to get an apple and a PBJ.

We meet Dominique's husband, Damien, and their two children. We sit with them in their modest garden at a table set beneath a fig tree, swagged with necklaces of twinkling white lights. Every so often, Dominique plucks a ripe fig and hands it to us.

This season, Ulli, not Monique, becomes the gravitational center of our social lives. In large measure, this is due to the fact that we have decided not to study with Monique. Why? We have difficulty distinguishing our reasons from our rationalizations. Because we have moved further east, it would take us at least forty-five minutes to get to her house. And there's the matter of money; the dollar remains weak against the euro. And then there's our perception that Mo has changed. There's a new love in her life. She has begun to invest modestly in rental real estate. She must look out for her retirement. We will visit with Monique, we will have her to dinner, we will delight in her company as always, but she will no longer fill our hours or jumpstart our social lives. Although I'm a Democrat and don't endorse the Republican theory of trickle-down economics, I do favor my own theory of trickle-down fluency.

We're convinced that if we stayed here for six months in a row, just wandering around, without even taking lessons, we will become something resembling fluent.

We spend a lot of time window-shopping, or what the French more aptly call "window licking." Wouldn't you know it would have something to do with tongues? We venture into particularly appealing stores, hoping to strike up a conversation. Each of these forays is an opportunity to prop up our French. I learn how to say "zipper," "Will the waist band stretch?" and "Do you have this in a large?"

One week into our sojourn, we are smart enough to realize that without some focus, without some order to our days, we will be in danger of slipping into our very own version of continental drift. We find a French teacher. She comes highly recommended. Her name is Solange Brihat. She lives in Bonnieux. We can walk to her house.

Studying French for two hours, two days a week serves as a much-needed organizing principle. The fabric of our lives this month feels flimsier. The minimal routine of our lessons keeps the threads from unraveling altogether.

We were right to soldier on in our pursuit of fluency. Mme Brihat is a very good teacher. She looks like Joanne Woodward. She is married to Denis Brihat, an internationally acclaimed naturalist photographer. He looks like Santa Claus. We study with her twice a week for two hours, seated at her dining room table in a lovely room full of books and art.

Her home, her husband's work, and her pleasant manner make us want to know her, but she maintains a professional demeanor. She doesn't offer conversation and lunch—even for a price—nor does she make any effort to introduce us to the community. We like her, and we sense she likes us, too, but, not surprisingly, she's doesn't want to be friends. She wants to be our teacher and get paid, just like teachers in real life. We call her Madame. We look forward to our lessons. Our French improves.

About midway through the month, Madame wonders if we'd like to take a daylong tour of Aix en Provence. Her fee is reasonable, and we're always up for something new, especially if it takes us out of the classroom. We fail to realize that being out of the frying pan will catapult us right into the fire. We will have to speak and be corrected for an entire day—a rare opportunity to suffer, learn, and enjoy.

Larry and I were in Aix three seasons ago, but our visit, because we're lazy tour snobs, was superficial. We visited the university and wondered carelessly about whether we'd like to study there the following year. We even picked up some brochures. What's a fantasy without brochures? We stopped to listen to two musicians playing Baroque music next to one of the city's many fountains. We had a coffee on the main drag, Le Cours Mirabeau.

At that time, we were nearing the end of our first season in the Vaucluse and had been thinking about what kinds of authentically Provençal gifts we might bring home to our friends. Other friends who have visited Provence have already gifted them with enough patterned cloth sachets of *herbes* de Provence to last a lifetime. Surely there must be something else. As we walked about, we couldn't help but notice the profusion of boxes of inexpensive cookies, called Calissons d'Aix, on display at the numerous souvenir shops we passed. Monique had once suggested that these cookies made very nice house gifts. They were, she explained, cookies with a fascinating past.

In the fifteenth century, Good King René, Provence's last ruler, wanted to give his future wife something unique, so he ordered his *pâtissier* to invent a special treat. The baker created a *calisson*, an almond-shaped cookie, made, not surprisingly, with almonds and studded with candied melon and orange peel.

We bought a few tiny boxes, one for ourselves and the rest for our friends. When we got back to Saumane that year, we opened up our box to take a taste. Or tried to. The *calissons* were stale—rock hard, actually, very fifteenth-century, very authentic.

A visit to Aix with Mme Brihat is different and fascinating. Mme Brihat knows her historical and architectural stuff. She walks us through the concentric rings of this originally Roman city. Like the rings of a tree, each circle tells its age. Collectively, they demonstrate how the architecture changed as the city developed toward le Cours Mirabeau. We make a quick stop at the Musée Granet, the walls of which should be but are not hung with paintings by Cezanne, perhaps Aix's most famous citizen. The largest collection of Cezannes is far from home, at the Barnes Collection in Philadelphia.

Madame suggests we return to Bonnieux by the Route de Cezanne so that we can see *la montagne* Ste.-Victoire. Approaching it from Aix on a winding road, one catches periodic, dazzling glimpses of the mountain, the bright sunlight illuminating the white limestone of its highest ridges. Each brief sighting builds our anticipation until, after a final turn in the road, we are rewarded with a full view of the mountain in all its massive glory.

La montagne Ste.-Victoire, in spite of its name, seems more like a craggy, gigantic boulder that has been placed on the landscape than a mountain that has erupted from the ground.

It is 3,317 feet high, half the altitude of le Mont Ventoux, but its base extends over eleven miles. It crouches majestically alongside the highway, its weathered limestone bare of all greenery, except at its base. It is one of the most stunning, natural sites I've ever seen. Perhaps part of its wonder is that we are seeing it up close. La montagne Ste.-Victoire so demands my attention that I don't want to leave.

No wonder Cézanne was obsessed by it, painting over one hundred versions from all angles, in all weather, in all seasons, and at all times of the day. We pay homage by taking about ten photographs and then reluctantly get back into the car and head for home.

CARUSO IN THE KITCHEN

Larry has found a recipe for *joues de porc* (pork cheeks) that has over ten ingredients, marinates over night, and takes most of the next day to prepare. He pays a visit to "his butcher," M. Isnard, to order the pork cheeks. Upon arriving in any town, Larry's first stop is *la boucherie*, where he likes to chat up the butcher. On an earlier visit, they bonded over the subject of worldwide sanitation rules and how "they" are making it impossible for the French to export or import certain foods, including Larry's favorite semisoft cheese, Reblochon, that, because it's not pasteurized, is banned in the United States.

"How are you planning to prepare it?" the butcher asks. Larry answers him in French that is comprehensible enough to engage the interest of the women shoppers who are standing behind him, waiting their turn. The butcher advises Larry to flour the cheeks before braising them. That way the sauce is thicker. One of the women volunteers that she cooks her pork cheeks for three hours; another says two and a half is enough. A third says that she marinates the meat the night before in red wine. Another serves hers with steamed potatoes. The customers are in no hurry to place their orders; they are far more interested in talking about Larry's meal. Larry wonders what he should serve for dessert. About this there is agreement. Figs are in season. Cut them into star shapes and place a dab of vanilla ice cream in the middle and add a splash of brandy. There's a woman at the foot of the hill who sells artisanal ice cream. Nothing less will do.

It occurs to me that this is my fourth stay in Provence and I have not yet heard anyone say "calories," or "cholesterol," or even "arterial plaque." The French do not season their food with regret, at least not here in Provence, the birthplace of French cuisine.

However, it is also true that more and more French people are like Americans—solitary fast-food eaters, stuffing themselves with quick take-out calories, followed by periodic dieting. *Le régime*, a diet, the word that once dared not speak its name, has now worked its way into the vocabulary, along with Jennie Craig and McDonald's, which the French familiarly called "McDo."

In 1999, a French sheep farmer named José Bové drove his tractor into a partially constructed McDonald's restaurant in Millau, a midsized town just west of Provence, thereby striking the first blow against what the French call *malbouffe*, or junk food. He needn't have bothered.

There are now at least 1,200 McDonald's franchises in France, second only to their number in the United States. On the Champs Elysées in Paris, the golden arches of McDonald's compete with the Arc de Triomphe. There's a McDo in the Louvre, and the *Mona Lisa* is still smiling.

The French franchisers of McDo have designed the restaurants and the menu to suit French tastes. Upholstered chairs invite the French to linger; the Mcbaguette Burger transforms a Big Mac into haut-ish cuisine.

The McDo-ing of France may be its culinary undoing, but in the small towns around us, the table still comes first. When Ellen enrolled her eldest child, Anna, in school, the principal instructed Ellen to bring *une serviette*. Because Ellen was still new to the language at the time, she looked up the word, learned that it meant either "towel" or "napkin," and sent Anna to kindergarten with a towel. The principal, who commands the norms of etiquette, had a napkin in mind. It should be brought to school clean on Mondays and retrieved on Fridays to be taken home and laundered. Fastidiousness didn't stop there. Anna, along with all the other children, was provided with a pair of delicate slippers to be worn at school, except during recess.

Anna spends at least an hour eating lunch at school, where the children enjoy a three-course meal of salad, fish or meat, and dessert. There are no trays, no cafeteria lines, no twenty-minute lunch periods, at least not yet, at least not in these small towns. The children sit in small groups around tables, where they are encouraged to help themselves and their tablemates to each course, to pass the bread, to take only their fair share from the communal platters, and to engage in conversation. This leisurely scenario exists in contrast to the fuel stop of a lunch at Anna's school in San Raphael, California. American children are, in effect, taught to rush, to wolf down their food, and to separate the idea of eating from the pleasure of socializing. Here, civility and sociability are taught at the grammar school table.

When Larry cooks, he likes to listen to opera, preferably bel canto. He turns the volume way up, like a teenager, and sings along. This house, like all our medieval rentals, comes equipped with a television, CDs, and DVDs, among which he finds one of his favorite operas, *La Bohème*. He is on such familiar terms with it that he calls it *La Bo.*

"Che Gelida Manina"—"What cold hands," Larry sings loudly to an imaginary, freezing cold Mimi, the tubercular love of his life. Blending his voice with Placido Domingo's, he doesn't sound half-bad. He gets so carried away by the infamous high C, the note that even Caruso was reluctant to attempt, that he sets his knife down in order to fling out both arms without causing injury.

Fresh from his triumphant visit to the butcher, he is also in the mood to speak French. If he doesn't know a particular word, he speaks English with a French accent, like Charles Boyer. "*Choppez et donnez-moi* zee parsley," he says.

In Provence, I often act as Larry's sous chef, chopping, grating, scraping, melting, and unrolling nasty little anchovy tins. I hand him knives, spoons, and parchment paper. I create neat little bowls full of carefully measured ingredients, and I place them on the counter in the order in which they will be needed. The French call it *la mise en place*.

The final moments of food preparation are conducted with solemnity and precision, as if we were in an operating theater. Larry stops singing.

"*Romarin*," Larry says, and I hand him the rosemary.

"*Estragon*," he says, and I slap two sprigs of tarragon into his waiting hand.

Larry adds and stirs. Mimi coughs.

When our meal is fully cooked and the sauce is reduced, Larry transfers the cheeks gently to a platter, sprinkles the dish with chopped parsley, gets out his camera, and takes a picture of dinner. Larry celebrates all our meals with a photo. He takes more pictures of his dinners than grandparents do of their grandchildren.

Pork Cheeks

Ingredients to serve 6

12 pork cheeks (Not easy to find in an American butcher shop, but a fancy one will have them or get them for you. They're very inexpensive, possibly because nobody but you even wants to think about eating them.)

1 bottle red wine; a Côtes du Rhône or other complex wine

1 carrot, peeled and cut into small cubes

1/2 cup extra virgin olive oil

1 leek, leaves removed and cut into quarter-inch cubes

1 tomato, chopped into quarter-inch cubes

1 onion, peeled and cut into chunks

1 clove of garlic, sliced

1 celery stick, cut into quarter-inch cubes

8 1/2 cups chicken stock

2 sprigs thyme

2 sprigs rosemary

2 sprigs tarragon

1 tablespoon brown sugar

parsley for sprinkling

Directions

Marinate the pork cheeks in the red wine for 24 hours. (Less is okay, but the butcher says the longer the better.)

Drain the pork cheeks, dust them with flour, and reserve the red wine. Gently sear the cheeks in heated olive oil. Then set aside.

Combine the carrot, leek, tomato, onion, garlic, and celery in a hot pan and caramelize on full heat. When caramelized, add the pork cheeks and red wine. Reduce the volume by about half.

Add the chicken stock, herbs, and sugar. Cover and slowly braise for three to four hours on low heat. When the meat is tender, remove the pork cheeks and set them aside.

Further reduce the sauce until it is very thick and with an almost firm texture. Pour sauce over the cheeks. Sprinkle with parsley.

(Note: This dish is excellent served with mashed potatoes, or pureed parsnips, or a hunk of crusty bread to sop up the extra sauce. Otherwise guests will be tempted to drink it from their plates.)

LARRY TAKES A MISTRESS

There's Larry, there's me, and then there's this third entity we bring along with us wherever we go, our marriage. At home, we're separated every day, except on evenings and weekends.

While planning our Provençal adventure, neither of us had thought about what it would be like to be together all day. We must have assumed that we would enjoy an enhanced sense of excitement at the happy prospect of more time together. We forgot to imagine that the problems that usually languish, almost unnoticed in the background at home, would move foreground in Provence.

There aren't a lot of things we don't like about each other in real life, but to come upon them on a fantasy vacation is particularly galling. How do we annoy one another? Let me count the ways.

Larry wakes up happy, a condition I find quite jarring first thing in the morning. He does the crossword puzzle, drinks coffee, sings in the shower, shaves, dresses for work, skips breakfast—"I'm not hungry"—and then stops at the doughnut shop on his way to the office. (I have a spy.)

I wake up drowsy. I don't mind that he doesn't pay any attention to me in the morning. I am not worth paying attention to. I want to be left alone to suck on my coffee until I am fully conscious. Meanwhile, I flip through the pages of the newspaper, scanning the apocalyptic headlines. Will it be nuclear war, terrorists, plague, out-of-control population growth, or global warming that does us in? The more I read, the worse I feel, the more sure I am that the world is coming to an end. Then I walk down the hall to my office and write humor.

There is nothing about this mutually exclusive routine that works in Provence. I can't wake up any faster, and Larry can't stand waiting for me. He's restless. Our different morning rhythms torment us both until, after days of urging me on, Larry realizes that if he took a long walk each morning, he could leave me in peace and smoke cigarettes with impunity, like a real Frenchman.

I am bossy. I love to tell people what to do, whether they've asked for my advice or not. Even people who like me think I'm bossy. My friend Gloria gave me a decorative wooden plaque, which rests on a windowsill in my office. It reads, "I'm not bossy. I just know what you should be doing." My compulsion to give advice is unstoppable. The only way to shut me up is duct tape.

Oddly, Larry the lawyer, a man whose profession is about giving advice, never offers me advice unless I ask for it. This courtesy, however, doesn't stop me from minding his business whenever I get the urge. When we're at home, he handles my bossiness with remarkable compliance. I tell him what he should do, and he does it, unless he doesn't want to.

In Provence, however, he finds me overbearing, no doubt due to an excess of togetherness. He experiences me as conducting a nonstop game of "Mother May I," demanding his obedience to the childish equivalent of giant steps, baby steps, backward steps, and umbrella steps. (Umbrella steps, as you may recall, involve twirling.) "Let's shop, eat, do homework, read, ride bikes," I command. He protests by throwing the game. He refuses to obey.

For my part, I suffer from fear of finding. Although I have never been in a paper bag, it is likely that I could not find my way out of one. My inability to navigate isn't much of a problem at home, but it moves front and center in Provence, where I'm totally disoriented and utterly dependent upon Larry, the human GPS, to show me the way. Larry doesn't mind. He loves to drive, and he enjoys being in control.

But I mind. How can I take myself seriously as a cultural adventurer if I don't have the guts to get behind the wheel of a foreign car in a foreign country, with foreign road signs and aggressive, tailgating French drivers, and risk crashing into something foreign? And I call myself a feminist?

Larry is very solicitous about my need to find my own way. Whenever I gather up my nerve and tell him I'd like to drive, he martyrs himself cheerfully and moves over to the passenger seat, knowing that he will lose all control and that, having lost control, he will clutch the console for dear life and impotently stamp his right foot on a nonexistent brake pedal. Such is love. He must be constantly vigilant, give me directions, boost my morale, and at the same time suppress any yelps of fear that threaten to escape his mouth. Little by little, I regain at least some of the premarital independence I enjoyed but gave up all too gladly, along with my maiden name, when I realized I had married a man who knew where he was going.

Larry is an obsessive compulsive. In a kinder time, one less inclined to make a pathology out of every behavior, he might have been described as a devoted worker. At home, his obsessive behavior is a minor problem. He changes lightbulbs during dinner. He throws away any unimpressive pieces of snail mail, like theatre tickets. He saves his best obsessing for the office. Until now. Unfortunately, Larry has brought his work to Provence in the form of his mistress, Mlle. BlackBerry. At home, she's not much of a problem for me because most of the time she and Larry stay at her place, at work.

I understand that if it were not for her, Larry would not be able to stay in touch with his office, which, I concede, he must do in order for us to afford this idyll, but I do not concede that he has to take her everywhere we go and be available to her at her every beck and beep. He always keeps her turned on. I can hear her vibrating in his pants. I beg and complain and nag and nag and don't get anywhere.

"I don't see what it has to do with you," Larry argues.

"That's just the point," I snap back. "When you're with her, you're not with me."

Larry insists that he can't live without her. "All these e-mails are emergencies, clients who must be serviced or at least mollified," he defends. "I've got to keep it on."

I don't believe him. What I believe is that he leads her on. It's not her fault. The more e-mails he answers, the more e-mails he generates. Why not bother your lawyer with unnecessary questions that can wait a couple of weeks until he gets home when your lawyer is crazy enough to indulge you in a matter of minutes?

As the days go by, Larry's relationship with his BlackBerry becomes more and more intense, and I grow angrier and angrier. Soon, his mania intrudes into the most private parts of our private life, the bedroom. First thing in the morning, upon awakening, he reaches for her and turns her on. He sits at the edge of the bed like Rodin's *Thinker.* "There's a six-hour time difference," he reminds me. "E-mails have been piling up during the night."

I try a reasonable approach, never a good idea with a stubborn man, but I keep hoping. "Set aside some time each day to answer all your e-mails at once," I suggest, as if he were seeking an answer. He says he will, but he doesn't. The e-mails come faster and faster. I continue to nag. I should know better. Nagging, like begging, doesn't work. It is woman's weakest weapon. At critical moments like this, a feminist doesn't ask, she takes.

"I'm taking the phone and putting it in my purse, turned off. I'll give it to you at the end of the day, and you can answer all your e-mails at once. End of story."

But that doesn't work either. When my back is turned, he riffles through my purse and grabs her. I realize that I am dealing with a high-textosterone e-mail addict. He can't help himself. The situation calls for an intervention.

"Either she goes or I go," I hear myself say with soap operatic conviction. The ensuing pause is not flattering, but he agrees. He will trade in his BlackBerry for an international cell phone with no texting capacity.

Suddenly clients are not so interested in communicating with Larry Lawyer because the six-hour time difference prevents easy access. People call only in the case of emergencies. The phone rarely rings.

Larry will endure days of withdrawal symptoms like phantom texting: tapping his fingers on tabletops and reaching into his pocket whenever a truck backs up, but in time, the addiction loosens its grip. Sometimes Larry will flip his cell phone open to give himself a quick hit of its dull yellow light, but essentially the crisis is over. The marriage is saved.

I make my own annoying contribution to domestic blips. I am very competitive. At home, where he's a lawyer and I'm a writer, we rarely find ourselves in competitive situations unless we're cycling uphill or playing Scrabble. No matter how many times I tell myself that it's how I play the game that counts, not whether I win or lose, I don't act as if I believe me. Larry swears that he doesn't mind losing—in court, yes, but not at Scrabble—and I don't believe him either.

AN ILL WIND THAT BLOWS NO GOOD

We become regulars at Le Restaurant St-André, just a short walk up the hill from our house and across the street from what has become our *pâtisserie*. The food's not that great, but it's inexpensive, and *le patron* is very friendly. Whenever he's got a dull moment, he wanders over to our table to chat.

On our first visit to the restaurant in early September, *le patron* warns us that the mistral is on its way. He predicts with great certainty that it will blow around the Vaucluse for the next three days. Sure enough, by the next day the wind is so strong that he is clinging fiercely to his outdoor wooden menu board while we clamp our knees on our napkins and hang on to our flatware that is doing a slow creep across the table. The mistral is well known for slamming shutters, nudging people, blowing swifts off course, and making people act crazy.

The word *mistral* derives from the medieval word "masterly." The constant hard, cold wind that blasts in from the north at speeds as high as fifty-five miles per hour depresses some people. Others become nauseated, irritable, and lethargic. Because Provence is so dry and sunny, mistrals spread fires that destroy acres of forests annually. On the plus side, they clear the air of dust and pollution and literally blow the clouds away. Indeed, the clarity of the air is one of the factors that attracted impressionist artists like Van Gogh to Provence. On the minus side, Van Gogh cut off a piece of his ear during one mistral and committed suicide during another.

We retreat to our house. Walking is nearly impossible. Biking is out of the question. Mme Brihat has warned us. Even though I'm wearing glasses, my eyes fill with grit. Walking home, leaning in against both the cant of the street and the opposing force of the wind, we barely make it to our front door. Once inside, I notice that Larry's Lycra biking shorts, which I'd hung on the ramparts to dry, are gone. I propose that we take a quick run around the neighborhood. Larry defers. "There's no point in looking for them. They're probably in St. Pants by now."

The mistral is not like any wind we've ever heard or experienced. Once I'm safely indoors, I like it. It sounds like a monster sighing: whew, whew, whew. Its force bends trees and wraps around the house. Its song climbs the scale from a slow bass rumble, like drumming thunder, to a breathy, whistling, mournful soprano. The mistral will return prematurely many times this September, driving us indoors, forcing us to relax.

How did *le patron* know precisely when the mistral would arrive? The answer is *La Météo*, the weather report. The French in general are preoccupied with the weather, no doubt because French weather is so variable. But there's more to it than that. The French have a snobbish attitude toward weather; they don't think that nature should inconvenience them. This may go some way toward explaining why those who report the weather tend to play to their audience in tones of shock and disbelief, as if snow in winter were an unexpected calamity or rain an absurd surprise. Even the press makes fun of their countrymen's weather obsession, calling them *"météo-dependent."* They treat television weatherwomen like rock stars. One channel runs a competition for Mlle Météo. The Provençales are even more *météo-dependent* due to le mistral.

Sure enough, after three days the mistral blows itself out, just as the proprietor of Le St-André predicted, and we venture out. So does M. Giles the elder, who, along with his retired cronies, takes his place against the wall. They don't even bother to greet one another with the preemptory *"Ça va."* Instead, the most urgent subject on everyone's agenda is the weather. *"Quelle horreur!"* they complain. The first words out of the butcher's mouth when Larry visits his shop are *"Quel temps de merde!"* The butcher wants to know how Americans say that.

"What shitty weather," Larry says, who by now has become quite expert on the various idiomatic uses of *merde*.

Monique claims there's a conversational hierarchy in Provence: first the weather, then murders, thefts and break-ins, and finally personal problems. But there's one exception. It is considered gauche to talk about the weather at dinner parties. Those occasions are reserved for violent political disputes. And one more weather alert: the Provençaux do not take kindly to outsiders who complain about their weather.

THE UNCOMMON MARKET

French supermarkets no longer hold mystery or challenge; even the weekly outdoor markets that used to be so thrilling now feel repetitive. The scales have fallen from our eyes. We notice that the same vendors tend to make the rounds of the same towns.

Did we really think they only worked one day a week? Their faces are as familiar as their goods: the olive lady, the cheese guys, the wild strawberries, the lipsticks, the kitchen devices, the sausages, the gardening shears, the gleaming rows of bright-eyed fish, the rayon dresses, the *rôtisserie* chickens, and yet another large wicker basketful of heartbreaking, darling little puppies and piglets. Except for the *grattons* man, the market at

L'Isle no longer excites as it once did. We've gotten used to it. That had to happen. In the markets, every day is groundhog day.

"Too many tourists," Larry complains as he tries to make his way through the swirling crowds.

Four seasons ago, when we lived in Saumane, we used to shop in a nearby farmer's market held on the outskirts of Velleron, just off the main highway between L'Isle and Carpentras. Now that we live in Bonnieux, Velleron is about forty-five minutes away. Still, in this, our season of impending ennui, it's worth the trip. We blend into a press of locals, baskets in hand, waiting behind locked gates. When they are opened, we run the gauntlet with the rest. The surge starts out frantic, like a potato sack race, but within a few moments the shoppers have dissipated and calmed down.

Perhaps as many as fifty local farmers drive their trucks onto a scruffy field and line them up in two rows, with the opened backs of the trucks facing one another, creating an aisle for customers as wide as a highway and as long as a New York city block. Some vendors don't have trucks. They set up their wares on tables. Some wear berets and the now faded traditional deep blue cotton jackets of French workers. Others wear aprons over T-shirts or conventional short-sleeved shirts. The female vendors, in contrast to their more stylish female counterparts in L'Isle sur la Sorgue, wear well-worn, unfashionable cotton dresses.

There are few, if any, tourists in the market today. Even though we think we blend in with the crowd, apparently we don't. It's the usual problem. Our clothes aren't quite right, and besides, Larry's got his camera out. He's photographing the merchants. What faces! The men's, especially, are tanned and lined from lifetimes in the outdoors, squinting at the sun.

"Their faces seem veneered," says Larry, "like faces in a Rembrandt portrait." Life often reminds Larry of art.

There's a policewoman at the market. She approaches us and asks if we're English. When people try to guess, they usually guess either English or German. That's probably because there haven't been many Americans in France lately. When we tell her we're from the United States, she gives us two thumbs-up and asks if Larry would please take her picture with me and the woman from whom I've just bought some apricot juice.

Larry explains to them that in the United States, when people are having their pictures taken, they say "cheese" in order to create the impression of a smile. "Cheese," he explains, is English for *fromage*.

"But don't say *fromage*," he hastens to add. Unfortunately he has confused them. When we develop the film, their mouths are hanging open.

Velleron makes the weekly markets seem faux. The fact that it doesn't open until six in the evening, in my eyes, adds to its legitimacy. I like to think that during that very day, the farmers were busy digging up their goods and loading them onto their trucks.

Some vendors—often the women—have only one or two items to sell: homegrown honey, melons, pumpkins, and somebody's special *confiture d'oignons*. Some trucks are packed with a variety of produce, eggs, and chickens. These probably belong to the full-time farmers. What could be more legit than buying carrots, soil still clinging from their threadlike roots, from a guy with dirt under his fingernails?

My attention is drawn to an elderly women, sitting behind a table, selling eggs from a woven reed basket. I recognize her from four years ago. Then she was standing behind a table loaded with purple grapes and peaches. Her arms were plump and sturdy. Her thick, pure white hair was twisted and pinned up in a neat knot near the top of her head. Her face was weathered, her features classic. I could imagine her finely sculpted profile in bas relief on a coin. She looked so striking that Larry took her picture.

Now she is sitting, her shoulders are bent, and a strand of her thinning white hair has fallen from her bun and lies against her cheek. She is thinner. Her hands are more gnarled.

I want to go up to her and say, *"Bonjour, Madame."* I want to tell her that I remember her. I want to tell her that I bought grapes from her, right on this spot, four years ago. I want her to remember me. But of course she wouldn't. I am connected to her by a fine filament of time. I have cast her in a drama of my own creation and given myself a walk-on part. I don't need to talk to her. It's better if I don't. For me she is emblematic of what is left of the real Provence I seek. Alain Prétot is my Provençal man incarnate. She is my rural Marianne.

We travel even farther afield to Arles in search of new marketing experiences. Most tourists go there to see the Coliseum, but at an entry fee of 35 euros per person, we settle for the view from the outside.

The marketplace is at least as extensive as the Sunday market in L'Isle. It starts at the Rhône River, where two lions on pillars guard the watery gateway to the city, and goes on for several long blocks.

Just when we'd thought we'd seen it all, Arles offers something new in Provençal marketplaces, a substantial Arab population. Their swarthy complexions, language, costumes, and customs add an exotic, foreign flavor that contrasts with the Gallic population that dominates the markets we have known.

At times it is difficult to move because of the shopping baskets, both handheld and rolling, and the profusion of strollers. Arabs love children and are inclined to have lots of them. They also like to stop and greet one another, which, when done the Arab way, holds up foot traffic. A "*Ça va*" spoken in passing won't do. First there is the requisite "Peace be upon you with Allah's mercy and blessings," spoken in Arabic. Next a double kiss, a ritual touching of the heart with the right hand, followed by lingering handshakes that must take place both upon meeting and parting. In between handshakes, it is only polite to inquire at length about the well-being of the entire family.

We get so literally caught up in the souk-like clusters of socializing Arabs that we never make our way to the food stalls. Instead, we are content to watch and admire their traditional, leisurely manners and enjoy the mysterious sounds of their language. We love being out of our element.

REAL LIVE TOURISTS

We are nearing the end of the month. We drive to Avignon to pick up our friends, Tracy and Gloria Sugarman. They aren't staying with us. They have rented a room in a bed-and-breakfast in Lourmarin, a tiny plus beau village near Bonnieux.

We are eager to reunite with these good friends and to show off Provence and our French selves. After all, Tracy and Gloria are guests in our country. They can't speak a word of our language—maybe *merci* and *bonjour* but not much else. They are depending on us to show them a good time.

We meet them at the Avignon hotel where they have been staying for the past two nights, touring the town. We assault them with triple kisses—delivered, *comme il faut,* left, right, left. Then we escort them to our car.

So far Tracy and Gloria have been having what most people would call a terrible time. Tracy his lost his wallet somewhere between the TGV railroad station in Avignon and the hotel. His wallet contains what most travelers' wallets contain—his credit cards, his driver's license, and all of his dollars and euros. He is a man without a country or a currency. Still, they are in the highest of spirits as we make our way toward Lourmarin.

Most people would panic, berate themselves, or, my personal favorite, berate each other, but the Sugarmans are not like most people, which is one of the reasons we like them. Both of them verge on pathologically happy. They were not going to let a total disaster get them down. It was nighttime when they arrived in Avignon. They were hungry. Luckily, Gloria had some cash.

They find their way to Le Bistro Lyonnaise, the place where I told my dud of a joke. Earlier, when we first helped them to plan their visit, we had urgently recommended the place. We assured them that the food was delicious, the atmosphere special, and that proprietor spoke perfect English.

"Talk to him," I had said. "Ask him if he remembers the woman who told the complimentary peanut joke."

They are greeted by M. Meduan, who does, indeed, remember the joke. Seeking an opportunity to speak English, he brings the Sugarmans their drinks, perches at their table, and engages them in conversation. It doesn't take long before Tracy tells the proprietor the tale of the missing wallet. M. Meduan is instantly sympathetic. He is determined to help them, especially after further conversation reveals that Tracy was a small boat officer during the invasion at Normandy during the Second World War.

So determined is M. Meduan, now "Yves," to help the Sugarmans that he closes the restaurant early and escorts them to the *gendarmerie* and the *préfecture,* just in case their property is retrieved, and then drives them back to their hotel.

"He couldn't have been kinder," says Tracy. "We had a wonderful time. Who says the French aren't nice?" We love that they love our countrymen.

First, we install them in their bed-and-breakfast in Lourmarin. We roll their suitcases down the winding, cobbled main street. The Sugarmans slow down to admire the cafés, art galleries, boutiques, the tea house, the bookstore—all the places we've enjoyed in seasons past.

"Albert Camus lived here," says Larry. "There's a street named after him, and he's buried in the local cemetery."

"Oh, let's go there," says Gloria.

"Let's get settled first," says Tracy.

Bernadette is the name of the proprietor of this shabby chic 1820s villa. We first encounter her in the magnificent walled garden of the villa. Old and bent, she shows us around the downstairs common rooms. They are authentically dark and decadent. In some places, the walls, which are crowded with paintings, are made of rough plaster. In other places, they are covered in patterned cloth dating from the Victorian era. The floors are sometimes stone and sometimes tile. The windows are covered in heavy linen drapes. Bric-a-brac and sprigs of faded lavender collect webs and dust on the shelves.

"Perfect," says Gloria.

All the while, we are speaking French to Bernadette. She is predictably impressed that Larry and I can speak as well as we do. Gloria and Tracy, who don't speak French, are even more impressed.

"Amazing," says Gloria. "We'd take you for natives."

"I didn't know you guys were fluent!" says Tracy.

"We're not really," I demur, but I am unaccountably delighted that they think we are.

Then we take them to our house. They love the three-story tower. They love ramparts. They love the kitchen, where Tracy hits his head. They love the view. Tracy, a professional writer and illustrator, can't wait to get out his sketchpad.

"The view is wonderful, wonderful," says Gloria, who gets redundant when she's happy.

"It *is* fabulous," I say, seeing it as if for the first time.

"See that crenellated castle over there?" Larry points straight out and a bit to the west. "That's where the Marquis de Sade lived; now the castle belongs to Pierre Cardin."

"And just wait until 9:06 p.m.," I say, picking up on the tour. "The tower lights up little by little over a period of minutes. It's breathtaking."

They can't wait until 9:06 p.m. Neither can we.

But first we meet Ulli at Le Fournil for dinner. Our delightfully impressionable friends are amazed to be eating dinner in a cave and pleased to see Ulli, whom they had met the year before, when she and Bettina were visiting us in Connecticut. They are happy to see one another again.

We are speaking English. Of course we are! It's our mother tongue! But somehow, with the arrival of our guests from America, we now think of English as our second language.

The Sugarmans want to take it easy on the first full day, so we take them to Saignon.

"You're going to love this place. It's one of our favorites—so peaceful and beautiful," we say as we wind our way up the hill. Being in the role of tour guides revivifies our enthusiasm for places we know well, so well, in fact, that we had been in danger of taking them for granted. We're going to love this place, too.

We introduce them to the statue of Ceres and then find seats at the outdoor café, where we enjoy our Oranginas and the view.

"Heavenly," says Gloria.

"Paradise," says Tracy.

"Yup," says Larry, as if he owns it. "Nice little place."

The pealing of bells from the church nearby interrupts our tranquility. It's a wedding! At least thirty formally dressed French men and women exit the church door, followed by the bride and groom. In an instant, we are on our feet, applauding the couple, mingling with the crowd. We take pictures of the newlyweds as if we were their relatives.

The next day, we head out on a nostalgia tour of our former houses. In Saumane de Vaucluse, we tell and show them the natal de Sade castle. They are enchanted. We tell and show them about how we thought Lou Clapas was a food chain and enjoy a laugh all over again. We tell about what an adventure it was to replace the broken glass shelf in the fridge.

In Goult, we order coffee at Le Café de la Poste. "That's where we lived," says Larry, pointing to the house across the way.

Ever since our guests have arrived, we have taken on new identities. We are French tour guides who speak English fluently. Our pretentions to be French have reached new and satisfying heights of faux-ness. We are experts on whatever it is we choose to show them, and we choose to show them what we know best and enjoy most about Provence.

We have coffee in Roussillon. Do they want to tour the ochre caves? They don't. They've seen enough for one day. We decide to go back to the house and rest on the patio before heading out for our dinner date at La Loube, which means a female wolf in ancient Provençal. The restaurant is located in the tiny town of Buoux, which rhymes with dukes.

La Loube is famous in the area for its authentic Provençal cuisine and the fact that it plays hard to get to, sitting, as it does, near the bottom of a canyon. The road to La Loube is nature's adventure ride—longer and more serpentine than any amusement park ride—and potentially fatal if you don't keep pumping the brakes as you negotiate the hairpin turns. Ten miles after crossing the highway, heading south, the landscape shifts suddenly from sunny, beige, and benign to dark and dangerous. Within minutes, you are deep into the tortuous canyons where athletes rappel down one-hundred-foot mountainsides that have been cut by time and the once torrential Aigue-Brun River.

Often the route is more tunnel than road. Projections from the limestone canyon loom and bulge above. In some places, they threaten to squeeze a car like a vice.

The first time we drove the canyon to La Loube, I was so terrified I inhaled, hugged my shoulders, and pressed my knees together in a ridiculous effort to make myself smaller. Larry gripped the wheel, gritted his teeth, and stared bravely ahead.

That was two years ago. The restaurant did not disappoint. The food was as spectacular as the trip. I particularly liked the way its ambiance complemented the feral, rustic environment of Buoux. The fact that our waiter looked a little lupine himself with his grizzled beard, sharp gleaming eyes, and large, pointy, canine teeth added to the allure.

Last year, the ride wasn't so scary, and the food was less appealing. Was I mistaken, or was the hummus a bit too oily? And the lamb—their premier dish—didn't seem to have that lovely taste of thyme that we had marveled upon during our first visit. We were pretty sure the waiter was the same guy, but he seemed to have trimmed his beard and had his teeth capped.

On this, our third trip down the canyon, the Sugarmans are appropriately awed by the tunnel of rocky horror. They duck. They cringe.

"Scary, isn't it?" I say, feeling their fear.

Gloria is a journalist. We met working together at a regional newspaper. We worked our way up from obituary to feature writers. Now she's a freelancer, specializing in travel and food. Gloria is so taken by the setting, the ambiance, and the authentic cuisine that she will write a rave review of it for one of her glossy food magazines. She has never enjoyed such authentic hummus. The lamb is the best she's ever eaten. We find we agree.

"Can you detect a little hint of thyme in the lamb?" Larry asks. They can. So can we.

"Lambs in Provence graze on it," says Larry, the French husbandman.

"By the way," says Tracy, when we're presented with the bill, "that waiter is one weird-looking dude."

The next day is Sunday, the Sugarmans' last day in the Vaucluse. A trip to the market in L'Isle sur la Sorgue is obligatory. Gloria spends most of her time in the antiques section where she nearly buys a hunk of an antique mantelpiece, considering it to be such a bargain at 10 euros that it's worth the price it will cost to ship it home. Tracy almost gives into her whim until he notices that it's actually one hundred euros.

We run into the Prétots. We triple kiss. We do the *Ça va* thing. Gloria and Tracy haul out their *bonjours*. Tracy has already made *Ça va* his own, so he throws that in for extra credit. We talk about getting together one more time before we leave. Sylvie suggests cocktails on Wednesday.

"C'est mon jour de repos," Alain explains, and we learn a new idiom. It's his day off. They'll invite Monique.

When it's time for the Sugarmans to leave, they have become slightly French themselves. They triple kiss. They've mastered *à bientôt*. We *will* see them soon. Our time in Provence is almost over.

AT HOME AWAY

How is it that one can seek out and respond to a life one has not experienced? Was Jung right? Is there a collective unconscious, some numinous mind to which we all belong? Are there primitive myths, patterns, instincts, and emotions to which we all subscribe? I recognize in myself a strong urge to find the beginning, to get to the bottom of things. If I were a physicist, I'd want to smash the atom. If I were an anthropologist, I'd dig for Lucy. In part, our protracted four-month expedition in Provence has been a determined effort to plunge backward in time to the historical essence of Provence. It is as if the closer we get to its Neolithic past, the more French we feel.

There is much that is foolish, superficial, even spoiled about our quest to rent-a-life. Still, it may be that our desire to make ourselves at home in Provence constitutes our own Jungian search for lost origins and authenticity.

Twenty-first-century life is increasingly isolating and inauthentic. We "friend" people we don't know. We express our feelings via emoticons. Robots solicit money and give us driving directions. Drones make war. We Skype our children because they live so far away. My granddaughter, Isabelle, lays her hand on the computer screen in Tucson, and I do the same, as if we were really touching. I think of the prehistoric handprints painted on the cave walls at Lascaux. It is the human thing to do.

Americans live closer to their history than Europeans, and so there is less mystery in our origins. A revolutionary cannon or an arrowhead unearthed in someone's backyard during a renovation is about as far back as we get. When the oldest churches in my New England town were built in the 1800s, the Abbey at Sénanque was more than seven hundred years old. I am greedy for age, for the way things were, for the way people lived.

Often when we're out for a drive in search of a breakthrough adventure, we play a game called "turn right, turn left." Today, we are heading home to pack on this last day of our month in Bonnieux. We're just outside of town when I see a small, wooden sign on the side of the road, one I hadn't noticed before, which points down a dirt road. The sign reads, *"L'Enclos des Bories,"* a borie village.

"Turn left," I command, and Larry does.

No matter how many times we see these bories scattered about the landscape, they never fail to deliver a jolt of excitement, an anachronistic clue to the mysterious past. They are as close to the origins of inhabited Provence as one can get. Some of them date from between the tenth and fourth centuries BC, when warring tribes were ravaging the valley, causing the inhabitants of the lowlands to take to the hills. What was it like to live in these dwellings? There is a borie village outside of Gordes, but it's so tarted up, so renovated, that it seems more Disney World than Neolithic. This borie village will turn out to be the real thing.

When the road gives out, we park the car and enter the village by foot. We are explorers, not tourists, if one overlooks the entry fee, which, of course, we do. Luckily, we're the only people there, and the guide is full of exciting information, all of it imparted in such clear French that we understand almost everything she says and can soon imagine we are not just French but Neolithic or possibly Bronze Age inhabitants. (There is some uncertainly about when the first settlers of this village arrived.) The conditions are propitious for a major breakthrough.

The people who lived in this borie enclosure were self-sustaining. A large, stone-threshing floor evidences the fact that they grew wheat. They farmed vegetables, trapped foxes and hares, and hunted wild boar. They built cisterns, a well, an irrigation system, and gutters for the recovery of water. We see the pens where the villagers kept sheep and goats, and the square niches in stone walls where they raised bees for honey. Some of the *pierres sèches* walls have vertical stones on top to discourage penned animals from climbing over. We remember seeing drawings of those walls at Le Festival des Pierres Sèches in Saumane. She points out holes in the timeworn stone thresholds and indications that wooden doors once secured the entrances to these bories, to assure privacy and to protect homes from the frigid mistrals.

She tells us that the cypress trees—the tallest trees in Provence, the trees so beloved by Van Gogh—played a critical role in borie village life. If there was one cypress tree standing at the entrance to the village, that meant that travelers could find a welcome, a place to pause and refresh themselves. If there were two, the hospitality included something to drink and eat; a three-cypress village meant the medieval equivalent of a three-star hotel: good drink, food, and a place to spend the night. This explanation seems so wonderful that it verges on improbable.

She shows us some small bories, each with little window-like openings, placed strategically along the periphery of the village, allowing a panoramic view of the Luberon Valley. They are lookout huts for surveillance, to detect advancing marauders. Of course we already know that Bonnieux, Saumane, and Goult, the three *villages perchés* in which we have lived, were once defensive outposts, but now we see what they must have looked like at their inception.

These same outposts were probably first used by the Celts who inhabited this village between the eighth and fifth centuries BC. In the fourteenth century AD, when the pope organized a crusade against them, the Vaudois tribes took to these same hills. Six centuries later, these very outposts, these very lookout huts, were used by members of the French Resistance during the Second World War. Even today, an occasional hippie left over from the sixties will wander into the village and treat himself to a Neolithic sleepover.

For each of our four seasons in Provence, we had set to out to find *"la vraie Provence"* that exists in its quaint, medieval villages and to some very limited extent, we had. The Provençaux, themselves, have worked to keep their ancient architectural and cultural legacy alive and deceptively original, in spite of the inevitable transformative losses to modernity. What we have seen of Vaucluse village life is far less real than what visitors saw in the seventeenth century, or the eighteenth, nineteenth, or twentieth centuries. As American writer and Francophile Edith Wharton wrote, "Each later generation draws a new base line and finds it hard to imagine what has already been lost." Even more will be lost to visitors who come after us. But here, in this living museum of an outpost, we have been transported. These were the first communities, the first villages, the first places the earliest settlers called home. We have traveled from present to past and arrived at the place of beginning.

Our guide dazzles us with the details of borie life. I see the hives. I hear the bees. I can imagine villagers—people much smaller than we, who don't have to duck their heads to enter their homes—sitting down to a meal of bread, lamb, and legumes and perhaps an intoxicating beverage made from honey.

We stop in front of a rectangular two-story stone house, with one delineated square window on the second floor, where the residents slept. On the first floor is a doorway, taller than the usual borie doorways. This is one of the more modern dwellings in the village. Where the floor is now dirt, our guide tells us, it used to be terra-cotta tile. The living room was furnished with a crude table, chairs, cooking implements, and, of course, a fireplace. We stop at the threshold and poke our heads inside.

"Entrez," she says. *"Faites comme chez vous."* "Go on in," she says. "Make yourselves at home."

About the Author

Mary-Lou Weisman lives in Westport, Connecticut, with her husband, Larry. She attended Brandeis University and Bryn Mawr College. She began her career as a journalist and columnist for the New York Times. Between 1998 and 2004 she served as a contributing commentator on Public Radio International's Savvy Traveler, and wrote a feature length film for Paramount Pictures.

Her passions include her husband, Larry, traveling with her husband, Larry, writing, reading, teaching and, until recently, when her rotator cuffs shredded, long distance swimming.

Mary-Lou has a special flair for social satire, and for mixing humor with the most sober of subjects. Her first book, <u>Intensive Care:A Family Love Story</u> (Random house and iUniverse) is such an example. New Republic reviewer Maggie Scarf called this debut book "A classic." The late Erma Bombeck called her best-selling second book, <u>My Middle Aged Baby Book</u> (Workman Publishing) "A perfect gift for middle agers and those in denial." Mary-Lou's collected essays, <u>Traveling While</u>

Married (Algonquin Books of Chapel Hill) some of which first appeared in the New York Times Travel section, are pure satire. The Philadelphia Inquirer review compared this book's humor to that of Erma Bombeck. Mary-Lou's last book is a biography Al Jaffee's Mad Life, generously illustrated by Al Jaffee, (HarperCollins). Art Spiegelman called the book, "An unnerving biography with a moving graphic novel hidden inside it." Playing House in Provence: How Two Americans Became a Little Bit French, a memoir, is her fifth book.

CPSIA information can be obtained
at www.ICGtesting.com
Printed in the USA
BVOW03s0737141117
500378BV00001B/8/P